THE LIMITS OF BOUNDARIES

The Limits of Boundaries

Why City-Regions Cannot Be Self-Governing

ANDREW SANCTON

McGill-Queen's University Press
Montreal & Kingston · London · Ithaca

© McGill-Queen's University Press 2008
ISBN 978-0-7735-3464-3 (cloth)
ISBN 978-0-7735-3465-0 (paper)

Legal deposit fourth quarter 2008
Bibliothèque nationale du Québec

Printed in Canada on acid-free paper that is 100% ancient forest free
(100% post-consumer recycled), processed chlorine free.

This book has been published with the help of grants from the
Canadian Federation for the Humanities and Social Sciences,
through the Aid to Scholarly Publications programme, using funds
provided by the Social Sciences and Humanities Research Council of
Canada and the J.B. Smallman Publication Fund, Faculty of Social
Science, The University of Western Ontario.

McGill-Queen's University Press acknowledges the support of the
Canada Council for the Arts for our publishing program. We also
acknowledge the financial support of the Government of Canada
through the Book Publishing Industry Development Program (BPIDP)
for our publishing activities.

Library and Archives Canada Cataloguing in Publication

Sancton, Andrew, 1948–
    The limits of boundaries: why city-regions cannot be self-
governing/Andrew Sancton.

    Includes bibliographical references and index.
    ISBN 978-0-7735-3464-3 (bound)
    ISBN 978-0-7735-3465-0 (pbk)

    1. Municipal government. 2. Metropolitan government. I. Title.
JS241.S23 2008   320.8'5   c2008-903041-9

This book was typeset by Interscript in 10/15 Palatino.

For Pam

Contents

Maps

Preface and Acknowledgments

This short book is inspired by Alan Broadbent, the remarkable Canadian philanthropist who has done so much to promote the ideas of the late Jane Jacobs. Because I too have always been an admirer of Jacobs's work, I was eager to respond to Alan's careful invitation a few years ago to become part of the group that was promoting a "charter" for the Toronto city-region and, by extension, the restructuring of the Canadian federation. Yet in the end my colleague Robert Young and I failed to answer his call, and I would guess that Alan's suspicions were confirmed: academics are an overly cautious breed, content to analyze, theorize, and justify, but not willing to take risks by attempting to bring about real and necessary political change. If Alan did feel this way – and he was far too polite ever to say so – then his views of academics are totally consistent with those of his friend Jane Jacobs.

I do not expect Alan to agree with much of what follows. I hope, however, that he recognizes how important his ideas and actions have been to me over the past few years and how much they have made me think about the structure of the Canadian federation and the nature of city-region governance. I expect that much of this book will serve to confirm Alan's views about the nature of the academic enterprise, at least as it is practised by political scientists. I even expect that many of my academic colleagues will consider this book as too negative and too institutionally conservative. For me, the purpose of this enterprise is to assist interested and informed citizens to think their way through our collective political problems. How to structure our institutions for the effective governance of our city-regions is the problem that this book addresses.

Jane Jacobs did not believe in studying cities in the abstract. Neither do I. This book is abstract at times, especially when I necessarily discuss relevant work by other authors, but I try constantly to return to examples of real issues and problems in real cities. This book is not a case study of Toronto, but at various points, especially near the end, I focus on the Toronto example. I do so because Toronto is Canada's largest and most complex city-region and because for the past thirty years I have lived on its periphery in London, Ontario, never really knowing whether I was part of the Toronto city-region or not.

As best I remember, I first articulated the idea for this book while drinking beer on a Friday afternoon at Western's Grad Club. As usual, I was with my colleagues John McDougall, Leon Surette, and Bob Young. Their always provocative and enlightening conversation (especially from Leon, a professor of English) spurred me on, and John helped me begin my research on the origins and evolution of national boundaries.

I presented an academic paper on the subject in 2006 at the annual meeting of the Urban Affairs Association in Montreal. The paper appeared to spark no reaction at all.

Meanwhile, various individuals read all or parts of the evolving manuscript. Bob Young's diligent reading – with marginal notes on almost every page – was especially helpful. I am also deeply grateful for his leading a collective successful effort to obtain funding from the Social Sciences and Humanities Research Council of Canada (SSHRC) to study the multilevel governance of Canadian cities. Although this book is not part of the SSHRC project, the influence of the project can be found on almost every page.

Thanks also to Tim Cobban for introducing me to William Fischel's *The Homevoter Hypothesis* and to Tom Urbaniak for catching numerous errors (including my initial claim that France was to the east of Germany) and for reminding me that residents of Cape Breton have not always been happy to be Nova Scotians. Lionel Feldman also made valuable comments on an earlier version of the manuscript. Richard Vernon pointed me towards some crucial sources during the initial stages of my research.

In addition to financial help for publishing from the Aid to Scholarly Publishing Program, I also gratefully acknowledge the assistance of the J.B. Smallman Publication Fund and the Faculty of Social Science, the University of Western Ontario. The Smallman funds have been particularly helpful in supporting the book's maps, which were prepared with consummate professionalism by my cartographic consultant, Patricia Connor. Steve Zuppa at the Serge A. Sauer Map Library in Western's Geography Department provided a number of the boundary files needed for the maps.

At McGill-Queen's I owe a debt to Joan McGilvray for shepherding the manuscript through the complexities of Canadian scholarly publishing and for assigning Judith

Turnbull as its copy editor. Judith's many queries demon-
strated that she often knew better than I exactly what I
wanted to express.

I thank my mother, Mary Sancton, for continuing my late
father's practice of sending me weekly batches of newspaper clippings about municipal government in Montreal. I
also thank Pam, Rebecca, and Derek, each of whom has
helped me in various ways to experience life well beyond
the sometimes limited boundaries of the academic political
scientist. They know little of what is written here and are
certainly not responsible for my errors or omissions. Neither is anyone else.

THE LIMITS OF BOUNDARIES

Introduction

Because cities are becoming increasingly important as sources of innovation and wealth in our society, does it follow that their own institutions of government will become increasingly autonomous such that they will become self-governing? I argue in this book that, contrary to some recent claims, cities in Western liberal democracies will not *(which* and cannot be self-governing. Self-government requires that *province* there be a territory delimited by official boundaries. For cit- *is most* ies, the boundaries will never be static, will never be accept- *urban?)* able to all, and will always be contested. Boundaries fatally limit the capacity of cities to be self-governing.

It should already be apparent that in using the word "cit- ies" I am not referring to central-city municipalities that carry the name of their "city-region." (For example, when people think of "Toronto" in its global context, they do not normally think only of the territory within the jurisdiction of the munic- ipal corporation of the city of Toronto; they are thinking in- stead of the wider, continuously built-up city-region that includes surrounding municipalities such as Mississauga.) This distinction is the source of much confusion and difficulty. There are examples of populous city-regions comprising only one municipality, but at least for fast-growing city-regions, the boundaries of such municipalities will always be problematic. The much more common pattern is for city-regions to comprise dozens, or even hundreds, of municipalities. The dilemma at the heart of this book is simple. Making central-city municipalities – and perhaps also their surrounding suburbs – more autonomous does nothing except reify existing boundaries that are invariably seen as arbitrary, outdated, discriminatory, and irrelevant. However, focusing on the economic and social reality of a city means focusing on the city-region as a whole, and determining its territorial extent for the purposes of self-government is not a practical proposition. Why it is not practical will be explained in later chapters. In any event, I shall generally try to avoid constant use of the term "city-region" by using "city" to refer loosely to a perceived economic and social urban entity. Sometimes I shall use "city" to refer to a particular municipal corporation and its legally defined territory, but in such cases the context should make my meaning clear.

A book about why cities cannot be self-governing might seem unnecessary. A much more common concern is that cities are hardly self-governing at all and need relief from the dead hand of central regulation. I am highly sympathetic to such a concern but have become worried about the implications – and confusions – involving many of the arguments and the inflated rhetoric about more autonomy for cities. They take us down a path that, in my view, can ultimately be damaging, if for no other reason than that they divert valuable resources to fruitless undertakings, much like searching for the end of a rainbow.

The term "self-governing" requires explanation. It obviously would include any scheme that establishes a city as a sovereign state with membership in the United Nations. Singapore is frequently cited as an example, but as will be shown on more than one occasion in this book, it is not without its problems as a model for a self-governing city. Its historical experience would certainly be difficult to replicate. A self-governing city could also be a constituent unit of a federation. Almost by definition, the constituent units of federations have substantial autonomous authority over a wide range of governmental functions that are especially important to the governance of cities. Such functions include the regulation of the built environment, infrastructure, culture, and recreational facilities, public education, and health care. Hamburg and Berlin, each a *Land* within the Federal Republic of Germany, are classic and oft-cited examples of city-states within a federal system. Brussels and Madrid are more recently established examples. These cases will be analysed in chapter 4.

For the purposes of this book, my use of the term "self-governing" extends even to what is often referred to as "metropolitan government." Such governments are superimposed on municipalities within a city-region and are designed to provide a wide range of common local-government services and regulatory functions for the entire area. As we shall see in chapter 3, the academic literature on metropolitan government is extensive, much of it concerned with arguing the case for the establishment of metropolitan government as a distinct level of government within a multi-tier system (i.e., national, state/provincial, metropolitan, and local). Although various cooperative arrangements among municipalities within cities are obviously desirable and necessary, the argument advanced here is that genuinely multi-functional metropolitan governments are no longer feasible – if they ever were – especially for the world's largest and most important city-regions. The object of this book, therefore, is to demonstrate that city-regions cannot be established as self-governing entities in any one of these senses: as sovereign states, as units of federations, or even as multi-functional metropolitan governments. Not surprisingly, there are some exceptions to such a sweeping statement. As usual, the exceptions will help us understand the general rule.

The book's title, *The Limits of Boundaries*, deliberately alludes to Paul Peterson's influential work *City Limits*, published in 1980. Peterson seeks to demonstrate that urban political analysts encounter profound difficulties if they theorize urban municipalities as simply being sovereign states writ small. He argues that, because urban municipalities do not control their own currencies, tariffs, immigration, and other crucial economic tools, their politics differ fundamentally from the politics of sovereign states. For one thing, municipalities are dramatically constrained in their potential policy options by their need to compete economically with one another for tax revenue. For another, the limited nature of their politics prevents the emergence of the kinds of political conflicts experienced within sovereign countries, conflicts that usually help create a system of relatively stable and competitive political parties.

Peterson's book has been extremely controversial. His elegant account of how urban politics can be explained by the differences among what he calls "developmental," "allocational," and "redistributive" policies has been strongly contested. But, at a minimum, Peterson's work has forced conscientious scholars of urban politics to ask themselves if they are unjustifiably assuming away the features of urban politics that are inherently different from the features of politics at other levels of government.

My minimum objective is similar. It is to insist that urban analysts pay attention to the problems posed by boundaries. At the level of the sovereign state, I shall argue, boundaries can be and are accepted as constant, except in the most unusual of circumstances. In urban government, boundaries are always contested, except in the most unusual of circumstances. This basic fact dramatically limits the potential of urban governments to replace other governments as the main decision-making authorities for city-regions.

In making my case, I must first explore the work of authors who appear to support the notion that cities are becoming relatively more important in our political life and sovereign states less so. This is the object of chapter 1. Chapter 2 focuses on the relative permanence of the boundaries of sovereign states and of the constituent units of federations, while chapter 3, in contrast, describes the flexibility and uncertainty of the boundaries of municipalities and city-regions.

Chapter 4 examines contemporary city-states in theory and practice, the practical examples I offer all drawn from European federations, as such models have often been considered as especially relevant to Canada. Chapter 5 is concerned with how city-regions that are not city-states can relate to their respective central governments.

Issues about the governance of the Toronto city-region inspired this book. I initially raise them in chapter 1, but explore them more fully in chapter 6. In short, Toronto is treated as an extended case study of virtually all the issues raised in the book as a whole. Readers who know Toronto should keep its circumstances in mind as they contemplate the arguments that follow. Other readers will want to consider how the Toronto analysis applies to cities that are of particular interest to them. It is my hope that they will be assisted in doing so by the fact that throughout this book references are made to dozens of cities around the world, especially in Canada, Europe, and the United States.

1

Focusing on Cities

There can be no doubt that sovereign states have for a long time been the main institutions of our political life.[1] There can also be no doubt that cities existed long before sovereign states were ever contemplated and that, in some cases, the governments of many cities predate the sovereign states in which they now find themselves. Although arguments are occasionally advanced that, in theory, the historical rights of such cities trump the constitutions of sovereign states, the courts established by such states have, not surprisingly, been unwilling to accept them. In short, city governments are legally subordinated, one way or another, to the apparatus of the sovereign state.

In this chapter, I examine the work of writers who, in quite different ways and for quite different reasons, challenge us to shift our analytical focus from sovereign states to cities. My conclusion is that their work is ultimately unconvincing, primarily because in each case it fails to take account of the intractable problems created by the need to draw boundaries. The first such writer is the well-known urbanist Jane Jacobs. She is not especially concerned about sovereignty, but she does argue that each city-region needs its own currency in order to prosper economically, thus clearly implying that the dismantling of sovereign states as we know them would be economically desirable.[2] Writing as political and legal theorists respectively, Warren Magnusson and Gerald Frug are more concerned with the ability of communities of people to control their collective lives democratically. They both see sovereign states (or American state governments in Frug's case) as part of the problem and new mechanisms for empowered city governments as part of the solution. Finally, there is the literature on "global cities," written primarily by geographers and sociologists, notably Saskia Sassen. This literature is often cited by those who believe that city governments are becoming more important, but in fact it has virtually nothing to say about city government, either in practice or in theory.

JANE JACOBS AND HER TORONTO FOLLOWERS

Despite her profound impact on the way in which we understand how cities work, Jane Jacobs had remarkably little to say about municipal government.[3] She was, however, as a resident of Toronto, a vocal opponent of the Ontario government's policy in 1997 of amalgamating the six constituent municipalities within Toronto's upper-tier metropolitan government. Her position was that big municipal governments were likely to do worse than smaller ones and that, in any event, amalgamation would certainly not save money, which was apparently the provincial government's main objective.[4]

In *Cities and the Wealth of Nations* (1984), Jacobs is primarily concerned with how cities grow economically. But she is quite explicit that the territorial entities she refers to as "city regions" require much more ability to make decisions for themselves if they are to serve their economic purposes. For Jacobs, cities that are economically successful create their own city-regions. City-regions comprise the central city, its suburbs and an area "beginning just beyond … [the] suburbs [where] rural, industrial and commercial workplaces are all mixed up together." As one would expect, she states that city-regions "are not defined by natural boundaries, because they are wholly the artefacts of the cities at their nuclei; the boundaries move outward – or halt – only as city economic energy dictates."⁵ For cities to generate city-regions, they must be capable of replacing wide ranges of their imports "exuberantly and repeatedly."⁶ Anyone familiar with Jacobs's *The Economy of Cities* (1969) knows that for her the key to the economic dynamism of a city is its ability to start replacing items that it previously imported from some other city with items that it creates on its own.

Jacobs is confident in listing examples of cities that have city-regions (Tokyo, Toronto, Boston, Milan, Paris, London, Antwerp, Amsterdam, Copenhagen, Sao Paolo, Los Angeles, San Francisco, New York, Singapore, Seoul, Taipei, Hong Kong, Wuhan, and Shanghai) and cities that do not (Glasgow, Edinburgh, Marseilles, Naples, Rome, Dublin, Belfast, Cardiff, Liverpool, Lisbon, Madrid, Zagreb, Moscow, Rio de Janeiro, Buenos Aires, Montevideo, Havana, Santiago de Cuba, San Juan, Sapporo, Atlanta, Seattle, Manila, and Canton). But she tells the reader nothing about how she arrives at her conclusions. Consequently, it is quite impossible to know how she would draw the boundaries of her city-regions. For Toronto's, we learn only that "it simply peters out and halts on gently rolling land presenting no change in natural landscape"⁷ and that it includes the nearby cities of Hamilton, Kitchener, and Waterloo.⁸

If the existence of city-regions had no policy implications
for Jacobs, then the absence of any discussion of boundaries
would not be a problem. But in her chapter on "Faulty Feedback to Cities," she makes a convincing case that cities would
be better off economically if they each had their own currency
whose value was determined by a "free float" in relation to
the currencies of other cities. If we accept her basic argument
that cities are the generators of economic growth, then it follows that each city will be in different economic circumstances
at any given time. A city that is in a downturn in its business
cycle (Jacobs explains how business cycles in a country are
simply the sum total of all the business cycles of cities within
its borders) will benefit from a currency that is falling in value
because its exports will become cheaper for potential custom-
ers and its imports will become more expensive. Similarly, a
city at a high point in its business cycle will have a strong currency that enables residents to buy imports more cheaply.
Anyone familiar with arguments about now national currencies work will be familiar with such reasoning. The originality
of Jacobs's thinking is her argument that city economies are
real, while national ones are mere statistical artefacts.

Jacobs points out that most old European cities once had
their own currencies, long before the emergence of currencies
of sovereign states and even longer before the creation of the
Euro, which has happened since Jacobs wrote *Cities and the
Wealth of Nations*. Just as Jacobs no doubt deplores the Euro,
she applauds the one recent case where a city managed to obtain its own currency. This occurred with the separation of
Singapore from Malaysia in 1965. Jacobs writes: "Singapore
has to earn its own imports or it won't have them, and generate
its own exports or it won't have them, but appropriate feedback helps it do both and replace imports as well. Singapore is
a nice well-made piece of equipment with a mechanism to

carry information and trigger responses (its currency), and a responding mechanism (its capacity to produce), forming a sensitively self-correcting economic unit."[9]

Significantly, Singapore is an island (or, more accurately, an archipelago, dominated by one large island). Drawing its boundaries could never have been difficult. As I have already indicated, Jacobs considers Singapore to have generated a city-region. What she does not state is that Singapore's city-region includes the Malaysian city of Johor Bahru (JB, metropolitan population over 500,000), a twenty-minute drive to the north across the causeway. In fact, JB's shops attract shoppers from Singapore, whose strong dollar (relative to Malaysia's currency) makes goods in JB seem relatively cheap. This area of Malaysia is also the sole source of Singapore's water supply.[10] Similarly, but to the south, a forty-five-minute ferry ride takes tourists and Singaporean businesspeople to a recently developed beach resort on the Indonesian island of Bintan.[11] Singapore has clearly outgrown its boundaries and has expanded economically into two other sovereign states. So much for the "well-made piece of equipment" that is the Singapore city-region.

Jacobs logically suggests that, for countries with their own floating currencies whose main exports are city-produced goods and services (as opposed to natural resources and/or agricultural products), there will likely be one economically dominant city within the country because as soon as one city becomes more productive than the others, the feedback mechanisms provided by the currency will benefit the dominant city more than the others. Once this process has begun, it is self-perpetuating. She argues that a non-dominant city can best prosper by extracting itself from the currency being used by the dominant city.

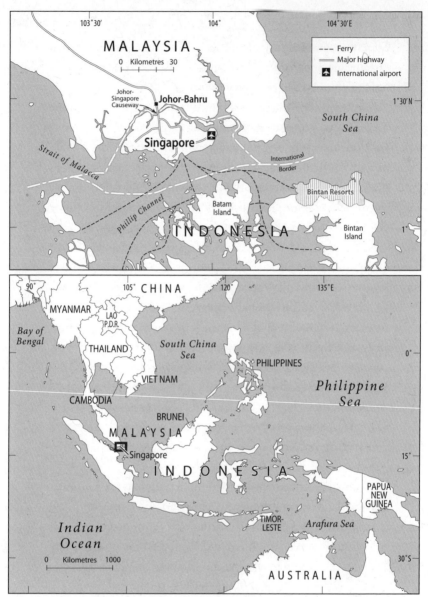

Map 1   Singapore and its links with Malaysia and Indonesia

    Small countries that are not city-states are in many ways
quite similar to Singapore. In her discussion of Denmark
and the Netherlands, Jacobs acknowledges this point.

Copenhagen dominates Denmark, even though it is on the extreme eastern edge of the country. In fact, since Jacobs wrote *Cities and the Wealth of Nations*, Copenhagen has been connected by bridge and tunnel to Malmo, Sweden, to the east, and the eastern terminus of the Copenhagen commuter rail system is now in Malmo. By any reasonable standards, the Copenhagen city-region now extends into Sweden.[12] Because both these countries still have their own currencies, the Copenhagen city-region is similar to that of Singapore in that it now transcends more than one sovereign state.

With respect to the Netherlands, Jacobs points out that the urban areas of the southern part of the country (including Amsterdam and Rotterdam) actually form a planned and integrated "Ring City" that "encircles the 'hole' formed by agricultural land and the inland sea."[13] for which, she implies, a single Dutch currency is quite appropriate. Now that the Dutch currency no longer exists and because the ring city is clearly not the dominant city within "Euroland," Jacobs's hypothesis would lead us to believe that the Dutch ring city will suffer economically having lost its most important feedback mechanism, its own currency linking it directly to the world economy.[14]

As with all of Jacobs's thinking about cities, her world view consists almost entirely of small entrepreneurs and independent consumers rather than of chain stores and large corporations. A separate currency for Winnipeg might do wonders for a small cabinet-making business, but it is unlikely to be popular among the shareholders of Winnipeg-based Great West Life or CanWest Global Communications, companies that do business across Canada and beyond.

The purpose of this discussion is not to assess Jacobs's overall argument about cities and currencies. It is to point out that if we have no idea about how to draw the boundaries of her city-regions, we cannot consider her city-regions

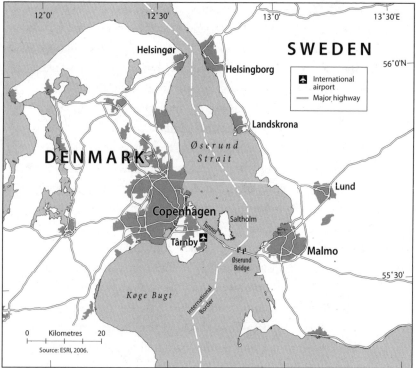

Map 2   Copenhagen and its links with Malmo, Sweden

as the territorial bases of a new way for promoting global
economic prosperity.

Influential as Jacobs's ideas have been, her 1985 writings
about city-regions might not merit so much attention from

students of city government were it not for the fact that her work has inspired a group of her followers in Toronto to promote her ideas as best they can within the real world of politics in Canada, Ontario, and Toronto. In 1997 this group organized a conference honouring Jacobs's work. She reportedly remarked at the end of the conference "that perhaps it was time for Toronto to separate from Ontario."[15] The group then went on to convene various discussions about the place of cities in Canada. In separate forums, the discussions have involved the mayors of five of Canada's largest cities (the "C5"), other representatives of civil society from the same cities ("C5 Civil"), and various intellectual and community leaders who have focused on issues relating to Toronto. It has been within this Toronto-based forum that more detailed proposals for a new political status for the city have emerged.

In 2001 the Toronto group adopted "The Greater Toronto Charter," whose first article stated: "That the Toronto Region form an order of government that is a full partner of the Federal and Provincial Governments of Canada, entitled to participate in discussions of an inter-governmental nature and in Canada's system of inter-regional transfer payments."[16] The remaining four articles very briefly outlined the functional, financial, and democratic responsibilities of the region. The boundaries of the region were not defined in the charter itself, apparently because David Crombie, a former Toronto mayor, warned the group that "people would waste all their time and energy arguing boundaries, and have nothing left for principles and policy."[17]

Writing in 2003, Alan Broadbent, the Toronto businessman who donated the funds for the group, provides remarkable detail about how he would restructure the Canadian federation. Each of his various options involves breaking up Ontario by creating a new "city-state of Toronto" whose

Map 3   The province of Ontario showing the Greater Golden Horseshoe

boundaries would attempt to capture the area generally known as the "Golden Horseshoe," the shape of which is formed by the western tip of Lake Ontario. As we shall see in chapter 6, in 2006 the government of Ontario officially defined a similar territory as the "Greater Golden Horseshoe." For Broadbent, the area stretches inland to Kitchener-Waterloo in the west and to the Alliston-Shelburne area to the north. He goes on: "Some thought has been given, by Jane Jacobs and others, to the creation of a new province of Southern Ontario, which would draw a line [sic] between Oshawa and Midland, and treat all of the Golden Horseshoe and south-western Ontario as a new

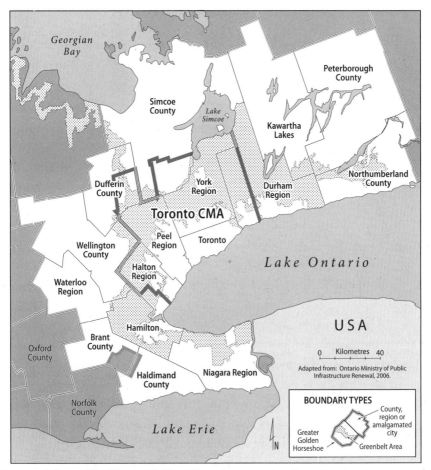

Map 4   The Greater Golden Horseshoe and other Toronto-related boundaries

province. This would have the advantage of including almost all of industrialized Ontario, including London, Windsor, and Sarnia, but would also include a lot of rural Ontario, particularly its prime farm land. However, on the principle of including similar areas within boundaries, this proposal does not work as well as a Golden Horseshoe based city state."[18]

By 2005, Broadbent's position appears to be moderating. He now asks only that "an expanded Toronto Region should have essentially the powers of a province" and that, although its "geography is arguable it likely includes the Golden Horseshoe around the western end of Lake Ontario.[19] In the same publication in which Broadbent makes this statement, another participant, Don Stevenson, a former Ontario deputy minister, writes: "An argument can be made that almost any proportion of Southern Ontario is Toronto's economic region but it is difficult to imagine any local accountability to a body beyond the limits of the GTA [Greater Toronto Area]"[20] – an area considerably smaller than Broadbent's Golden Horseshoe. Confusion reigns. Broadbent is referring to an entity that is to be like a province and Stevenson – and others in the group – is still conceiving the Toronto region as some form of metropolitan or regional government within the general paradigm of local government.[21]

In his 2008 book, *Urban Nation*, Broadbent advocates provincial status for the city-regions of Montreal and Vancouver, as well as of Toronto. Because reaching constitutional agreement on the establishment of new provinces would be almost impossible, he suggests that individual provinces could grant autonomy to city-regions such that they would have all the powers of the province, thereby creating a kind of province within a province.[22] He acknowledges that the "boundary issue is tricky,"[23] but claims that it can be overcome for each city-region by one of three mechanisms: arbitrary provincial legislation; determination by impartial appointed commissions or by the Senate of Canada; or the knitting together of the boundaries of various functional bodies – especially regional transit authorities – that have evolved incrementally over the years. It is clear that the second of these three options is his preferred choice.[24]

Broadbent's most startling suggestion, in light of his avowed commitment to city-regions, is that commissions charged with making recommendations about city-regions would do well initially to adopt boundaries that correspond to those of the central-city municipality, in the expectation that neighbouring cities would then opt in voluntarily. "The objective would be to have as much of a contiguous region as possible included."[25] In the rest of this book, I shall explain both the folly of relying on the central-city boundaries and the unlikelihood of neighbouring cities joining in such a way as to create a self-governing city-region with boundaries appropriate for solving city-region problems.

There can be no doubt that Broadbent's various radical proposals relate directly to his basic agreement with Jacobs's thought and the close personal connection between the two. In this context, however, it seems ironic that Broadbent has written nothing about the desirability of the Toronto region (however defined geographically or politically) having its own currency. For Jacobs, city-regions are to be autonomous precisely so that they can reap the economic feedback benefits of having their own currencies. There might be many benefits from establishing autonomous city-regions within Canada's provinces, but they are not readily apparent to the reader of *Cities and the Wealth of Nations*.

(How do currencies work?)

WARREN MAGNUSSON AND GERALD FRUG

Most of the political debate about the governance of city-regions has been dominated by "consolidationists," who want bigger local governments in one form or another, and the advocates of "public choice," who point to the economic benefits of smallness and competition.[26] There is very little theory about city-region governance that does not fall within one or the other of these approaches, both of which are more

concerned with the effectiveness and efficiency of local government than with fundamental issues at the heart of political and legal theory. Warren Magnusson, a Canadian political
theorist at the University of Victoria,[27] and Gerald Frug, a
municipal-law specialist at Harvard University, are exceptions, and that is why their work deserves attention. They
have both written important and theoretically sophisticated
books on the subject of urban governance: *The Search for Political Space: Globalization, Social Movements, and the Urban Political Experience* (1996) by Magnusson and *City Making: Building
Communities without Building Walls* (1999) by Frug.

Magnusson and Frug both require their readers to jettison
state-centred conceptions of political life. They argue that
the cities in which people live are the locations that are most
politically meaningful and that the larger governmental
units that contain them are artificial constructs whose actions limit the ability of city residents to manage their collective futures democratically. They understand that municipal
governments that are subordinated to, and managed
by, larger governments cannot come close to providing the
kind of active, engaged city government that both think
is necessary.

To understand what such a city government would look
like, consider Frug's list of six activities that "[c]ities committed to community-building" might undertake:

- operating banks and other financial institutions in the interests of promoting the regional economy;
- running a cable television system to enhance democratic
  communication;
- building or acquiring residential housing to prevent spec-
  ulative profit-taking;

- sponsoring cooperative grocery stores to promote demo-cratic organization and to help areas not well served by privately owned grocery stores;
- owning a major sports team so as to connect "the enthusi-asm for local teams ... with community-building efforts"; and, finally,
- supporting "community organizations devoted to easing the burdens of family life."[28]

The significance of this list does not lie in the pros and cons of each suggestion but rather in the fact together they illus-trates quite different ways of conceptualizing the role of city governments, viewpoints that are outside our normal frame of reference when we think about city governments in North America.

Frug attempts a thoroughgoing critique of mainstream ju-dicial interpretations of American local-government law. His main objective is to *decentre* local-government law by insist-ing that judges and legislators should not *centre* on the rights and obligations of each particular municipality, be it central city or suburb, but rather "situate" the law within its wider social and economic context. He therefore turns to city-regions as the main (but not only) centre in which local gov-ernments should be situated. He wants to establish "regional legislatures" to replace state legislatures as the source of au-thority for the municipal governments within city-regions. He writes: "The purpose of establishing a regional legislature would not be to enable it to act as a regional government ... [T]he task of the regional legislature would be to perform one specific function of the state legislature and the state courts: defining the power – specifying what lawyers call the legal entitlements – of local governments."[29]

Frug insists that the regional legislature would not act directly on regional residents. It would only make rules (legal entitlements) for local governments within its territory, rules, for example, about land-use policies, sharing of school taxes, locating waste facilities, offering tax incentives to businesses, and controlling guns. He acknowledges that the distinction between "the entitlement allocation function of a regional legislature" and that of a regional government is difficult, because the entitlements could be structured in such a way that local governments have no choice but to follow particular paths predetermined by the nature of the entitlements. Frug suggests that this problem can be overcome through the organization of the regional legislature: "The regional legislature, rather than the individual cities, must have the power to determine which questions it can decide. However, it should be structured to encourage its members not to exercise power themselves but to turn the legislature into a forum for interlocal negotiations about how to decentralize power. The best chance of doing so, in my view, lies in electing representatives from the geographical areas to which the people feel most attached – central-city and suburban neighbourhoods."[30] In other words, Frug wants the electoral arrangements for the regional legislature to re-enforce local identities, not to dissolve them in one common regional identity.

Frug's proposals for institutional change are at least as radical as those of Jane Jacobs and her followers. His approach leaves little room for state governments: "Regions are as diverse as states, and they therefore can serve the purpose of protection against parochialism usually advanced for state power. In fact they can serve it better. Because many metropolitan regions in America cross state boundaries, state decision-making often increases the fragmentation of metropolitan regions rather than reducing it."[31] Like Jacobs, Frug pays remarkably little attention to the boundaries of the regions with which he is so much concerned. In much of his book, he focuses on how to overcome the effects of boundaries among municipalities (particularly central cities and suburbs) that are excessively centred, but he does not even mention the boundaries of the regions themselves until the very last page, and then in the most cursory fashion. He suggests that the federal government has a special role to play in defining "metropolitan regions": "If it undertakes this responsibility, however, it must prevent regional boundaries from reproducing on a larger scale the current effects of city boundaries. The difficulty of drawing boundaries in many parts of the country should be treated as a virtue: from the neighbourhood level to the national level, the objective should be to reduce the impact that geographic boundaries have on people's lives."[32] In an endnote for this passage, Frug states that the "census defines regional areas and is therefore a place to begin."[33] Indeed it is – and the way the Canadian and American censuses approach this task will be discussed in chapter 3. But, for someone who is so sensitive to the issue of boundaries within city-regions, Frug is remarkably insensitive to the obvious fact that the process of drawing regional boundaries within his framework would inevitably raise huge difficulties of precisely the kind that he addresses throughout the rest of his book.

Warren Magnusson's work is in many ways remarkably similar to that of Gerald Frug. Magnusson's book *The Search for Political Space* appeared three years before Frug's *City Building*, but Frug makes no reference to Magnusson. In any event, Magnusson is just as concerned with "decentring the state" as Frug is, probably more so. The main difference is that Magnusson is not so centred on regions. He privileges no particular territorial configuration, analysing all of them, from villages and urban neighbourhoods to global institutions and social movements, in different political contexts. In so doing, he outlines what democratic politics might look like in the absence of state sovereignty.

Magnusson claims that at least some of "the literature on public administration" constitutes "an explicit attack on the locality as an appropriate political community." He goes on to address a set of issues that are so crucial to my concerns in this book that they merit a lengthy direct quotation:

> In a curious inversion, the locality (rather than the state) is thus presented as an *artificial* community. Since everyday life lacks definite boundaries, to impose boundaries for the purposes of local administration – establish a political container and say, "This is the locality" – does indeed seem artificial. We use services from hither and yon, and there is no natural area within which all our intermediate needs can be met. Communal loyalties spread over the region and beyond, but they contract toward the neighbourhood and the block. There is no agreed order of priority among these loyalties. Thus the container chosen for local government and politics is apparently arbitrary or artificial, in terms of both objective and subjective measures of community identity. As we have noted, one might say the same of the state and the national community it is supposed to maintain. Only by strenuous effort can governments render communities natural and inevitable which would otherwise seem highly questionable.[34]

For Magnusson, a vibrant democratic life is only possible if citizens are engaged in politics at all territorial levels – and if they understand, say, the connections between decisions of the World Trade Organization (WTO) and air pollutants that might be emitted from a factory at the end of their street. Citizens are not engaged at all in real politics if their focus is solely on the apparent leaders of a sovereign state. Unlike Jacobs and Frug, Magnusson has no particular brief for self-governing city-regions. He understands that there is no easy way to draw boundaries for city-regions, even though they constitute very important territorial communities for most people who live in cities. But Magnusson assumes that we can each simultaneously be part of a number of self-governing territorial communities, with the result that no particular boundary in itself is of crucial importance to the life chances of any particular individual. For Frug, however, someone is in charge of boundaries, whether regional legislatures for municipal boundaries or, incongruously, the federal census agency (as a starting point, at least) for the boundaries of the regions. For Magnusson, it appears that no one – or no institution – is in charge. The boundaries simply emerge from some undetermined process, the result being a deeply multi-level politics in which the concept of sovereignty is irrelevant.

In their own ways, Jacobs, Magnusson, and Frug want to eliminate the importance of governmental boundaries. This is quite explicit for Magnusson and Frug, less so for Jacobs. In Jacobs's ideal world, we would all be changing currencies as we travelled from one city-region to another, so it seems strange to claim that she too wants to eliminate the importance of boundaries. It must be remembered, however, that the sole purpose of having different currencies is

to equalize opportunities for economic growth and innovation in the longer term on both sides of any given boundary.
My argument here is different. I contend that, unless or
until there is a form of strong and centred world government, boundaries between states (and between federations
of states, including the European Union) will be of crucial
importance, not just for individuals, but for cities as well.
Such an argument must seem weirdly out of step, not just
with the work of Jacobs, Magnusson, and Frug, but with the
much better-known literature about how global cities are
displacing nation-states as the driving forces in the globaliz-
ing world economy.

GLOBAL CITIES AND CITY GOVERNANCE

We need not be concerned here with which cities qualify as
global and how best to construct the hierarchy of the importance of each in relation to the others. The key point is that
there is ample evidence that the world's largest cities are becoming increasingly linked to each other and increasingly separated from many of the concerns and issues that are relevant
to the small towns and rural areas in their respective countries.
Global cities and their immediate hinterlands prosper, while
more distant regions within their respective countries struggle
to maintain existing levels of employment and standards of
living. There is more and more evidence that "national economies" are exactly what Jane Jacobs has described them as: statistical artefacts. Most economic activity takes place in cities
that are linked to one another in complex networks of trade,
information flow, and shared cultural activity.

To the extent that sovereign states find it increasingly impossible or counterproductive to attempt to regulate such

connections among the world's largest cities, we can correctly conclude that sovereign states are becoming less powerful and less important, at least in relation to controlling what comes and goes across their borders. Saskia Sassen is well known for having documented the emergence of global cities.[35] For our purposes, the most important aspect of her work is what it omits: she has absolutely nothing to say about the government of the global cities she writes about. As Peter M. Ward has pointed out,[36] such an omission is common in the literature on global cities. The omission in itself is not a problem, because Sassen and her colleagues are interested primarily in analysing the linkages among global cities and the forces that cause them to share many crucial characteristics.

Kenichi Ohmae's best-known books are provocatively entitled *The Borderless World* and *The End of the Nation State*. They have been hugely influential in advancing the view that nation-states are declining in importance and that entities Ohmae calls "region states" are becoming more important. These region states are similar to Jacobs's city regions, although Ohmae tends to focus on regions that cross the boundaries of nation-states. Unlike Jacobs, however, he is not especially concerned with currencies. Indeed, he seems quite unconcerned with any public functions that these "states" may or may not perform, other than the functions of attracting foreign investment, encouraging economic innovation, and acting as a catalyst for the regions. Ohmae seems to favour loose federations of region states,[37] but he provides very few details about how such federations might actually work. He says nothing about boundaries. But, more than any other single author, Ohmae has popularized the notion that profound changes are occurring in the way we govern ourselves and that cities (or region states) are taking over.

Unlike Sassen, Ohmae actually does refer to sub-national governments. He is especially concerned with restructuring the Japanese state such that the centre becomes less powerful and authority is devolved to eleven regions whose boundaries would relate primarily to patterns of existing economic linkages. Ohmae sees the American and Canadian federations as models from which the Japanese can learn a great deal. He makes no suggestion that state and provincial boundaries in the United States and Canada are in any way artificial. In fact, he is suggesting that the region states within these two countries are the existing states and provinces.[38] From a North American perspective, Ohmae is not much of a radical, even though he is often cited as an important visionary who foresees drastic changes in the way we govern ourselves, changes that apparently have something to do with the increasing importance of cities and their regions.

Another important popularizer of the notion that cities are in the process of displacing nation-states as key actors on the world stage is Neal R. Peirce. In newspaper columns, consultants' reports, and an influential book, he urges that we think of cities and their surrounding regions as "citistates," which he defines as "entities that perform as critical actors, more on their own in the world economy than anyone would have dreamed possible since the birth of the nation-state in the 16th and 17th centuries."[39] Peirce's citistate concept is notoriously vague, often amounting to little more than business partnerships that are established to promote regional growth and innovation and that transcend municipal borders. Unlike Alan Broadbent, he is not much interested in constitutional change: "No one is suggesting that American state government give way to citistates, constitutionally or any other way. But the essential interdependence of the states and citistates has emerged as an indispensable feature of governance in the latter years of the 20th century."[40]

Peirce addresses the territorial scope of a citistate with a series of questions:

- Does the citistate encompass just the original core city and its immediate surrounding areas?
- Or, in US terms, all of a census-defined metropolitan statistical area?
- Or the viewing area of the city's television stations?
- Or the radius of the longest commute, which some would define as the citistate's "commute-shed"?
- Or virtually all the exurban, rural territory up to the orbit of another citistate?

He argues, as do I and many others, that it is precisely because of "the infinite variety of geographic configurations" of citistates that they are "the most dynamic form of human settlement today."[41]

Ohmae and Peirce are among the most sophisticated of the many consultants and popularizers of the idea that cities and their regions are somehow in the process of eclipsing nation-states.[42] Vague as their conceptual apparatus might be, they at least avoid some of the fundamental logical errors found among the less sophisticated camp followers of the global-cities literature. The error I am most concerned with starts from the established facts that the analysts of global cities have documented. It then proceeds as follows with two assumptions:

- Cities are governed by municipalities.
- Because cities are growing in importance, municipalities are (or should be) growing in importance, just as sovereign states are (or should be) decreasing in importance.

The second assumption about municipalities leads to all
kinds of fairly obvious policy recommendations, some of
which will be explored later in this book. The problem with
this reasoning is that cities are *not* governed by municipalities. It is true that municipalities are the level of government
whose territories most often encompass urban areas, but
municipal governments always share functional responsibility for such urban areas with other levels of government.
Usually other governments are in charge of the functions
that are of most importance to residents of the city: money
and banking, immigration, criminal law, commercial law,
public health care, unemployment insurance, and social assistance. Most advocates of increased municipal power
would not dream of transferring such functions to municipalities. Even Jane Jacobs does not want these functions to
be municipal. In *Cities and the Wealth of Nations,* she advocates that city-regions be constituted like sovereign states,
not that municipalities within such city-regions take on
functions that are usually the responsibility of sovereign
states. Once we recognize that municipalities will always be
only be *part* of a multi-level system of government for cities,
we will realize that there is nothing inevitable about the future role of municipalities. It might well be the case that as
cities become more important in relation to the functioning
of our economy, municipalities will actually become of less
relative importance.

2

Boundaries for Central Governments

The purpose of this chapter is to demonstrate that the boundaries of sovereign states are relatively stable and have become even more so in recent years. When new states have been created, they have generally used old boundaries, often the boundaries of constituent units within the state. In federations, these constituent units – states and provinces in the United States and Canada – generally have constitutional responsibility for local government. For municipalities in North America, the states and provinces are effectively the sovereign unit of government. For the purposes of this book, it is important that we understand that they are even more important than the federal governments based in Washington and Ottawa. In this chapter, we look at the boundaries of sovereign states and then at the boundaries of constituent units in federations. But first we explore some of the more theoretical issues relating to the boundaries of sovereign states.

THE OPTIMAL SIZE OF NATION-STATES

Robert Dahl is one of the few modern political scientists to have paid much attention to the relationship between size and democracy. He emphasizes that the first conceptions of democracy related to the city-state and that this vision "prevailed, by and large, from the Greeks to Rousseau."[1] According to this understanding, democracy involved debate among citizens in open meetings followed by a decision-making process in which every citizen had a direct voice. But this form of democracy eventually gave way to the kind of representative democracy we are familiar with today in our larger nation-states. Dahl is very much concerned with trying to balance the effectiveness of citizen participation, which is more feasible in smaller political units, with the capacity of political systems to accomplish collective objectives, which is enhanced in larger units. He arrives at no firm conclusions, other than to suggest that effective democratic governance requires governments of different scales – from the neighbourhood to the world – to achieve different functional objectives.

The most ambitious formal approach to the issue of the optimal size of nations was published in 2003. Albert Alesina and Enrico Spolaore "argue that the sizes of national states (or countries) are due to trade-offs between the benefits of size and the costs of heterogeneity of preferences over public goods and policies provided by government."[2] The authors carefully outline the assumed "benefits of size," claiming along the way that "the per capita costs of many public goods generally decline with the number of taxpayers."[3] But as countries get larger, and therefore more heterogeneous, "there are more individuals or regions that are less satisfied by the central government policies."[4] Such dissatisfaction can make decision-making more costly and difficult and in extreme cases can threaten the very existence of central governments.

In an analysis familiar to students of local government, Alesina and Spolaore point out that in theory we could organize ourselves politically such that we would be part of a different governmental authority for each different governmental function. Each authority would have the optimal territory for its own purposes. We would all then be subject to multiple "special-purpose bodies" with overlapping boundaries.[5] But such an arrangement would sacrifice economies of scope that result from having the same entity perform more than one function. The authors also point out that control over the legitimate use of coercive force "plays a special role"[6] that forms the defining characteristics of states. The existence of states puts them in a privileged position to take control of "a host of other functions for reasons of economies of scope or transaction costs."[7] Sovereign states are then also able to determine mechanisms for political decentralization.

Most of Alesina and Spolaore's book concerns the impact of trade regimes and defence considerations on the size of nations. Their formal modelling suggests that "democratization, trade liberalization, and reduction of warfare are associated with the formation of small countries, whereas historically the collapse of free trade, dictatorships, and wars are associated with large countries."[8] Such findings are consistent with the view that city-states are the wave of the future. Like Jane Jacobs, Alesina and Spolaore note the economic success of Singapore.[9] Unlike Jacobs, however, they say nothing about the particular role of cities in creating economic prosperity, for example, and they certainly do not tackle the issue of where in the real world boundaries should be drawn, be they around cities or anything else.

Alesina and Spolaore do address the issue of optimal currency areas, a subject about which, as we have seen, Jacobs had strong views. For them, the issue is very similar to that of the optimal size of nations, except that they assume there will be fewer currency areas than nations: "A common currency reduces transaction costs in trade; the larger the currency area, the larger are the benefits of scale (reductions of transaction costs). Money is like a common language: the more people use it, the larger the benefits of easier communication." On the negative side, however, they recognize that countries joining a currency area give up their autonomy to use "monetary policy to stabilize idiosyncratic shocks to their economies."[10] This, of course, is exactly Jacobs's point: why should two major cities share the same currency if the economy is booming in one and faltering in the other? According to Jacobs, the common currency will be delivering faulty "feedback" to each of them. The resulting economic losses would be much more than any gains that might have come from reduced transaction costs.

Alesina and Spolaore acknowledge the important role that political decentralization can play in enabling larger countries to remain intact. Such decentralization is "an intermediate organization form in between the maze of overlapping jurisdictions on the one extreme and the one-level-of-government-does-it-all on the opposite extreme."[11] When the authors refer to the heterogeneity of the world, which acts as a barrier to the infinite enlargement of states, they at least make reference to such factors as race, religion, and language.[12] However, in their discussion of decentralization, they make no reference to factors that might determine the boundaries of the decentralized units other than to state the obvious: "certain policies can be delegated to localities, in order to allow for local preferences."[13] Unfortunately, we are given no guidance as to what a "locality" might be. There is no reference, even in this discussion of decentralization, to cities.

SOVEREIGN STATES

In October in the year 842, about 120 "experts" (*omni nobilitate praesantes*) were gathered together in Metz to help determine how to divide Charlemagne's empire among his three grandchildren. According to one well-known interpretation of what happened, the division imposed by the Treaty of Verdun in 843 "was deliberately designed to allocate to each heir a share that took a fair account of the climatic conditions of the various zones in the Empire and their respective natural resources."[14] To accomplish this objective, three kingdoms were created, each of which bordered both the North or Baltic seas on the north and the Mediterranean Sea on the south. Such a division provided each heir with land in the north that was good for raising horses, land in the middle that was good for the production of cereals and other food-crops, and land in the south that was suitable for the cultivation of the trees and vines that were used for making olive oil and wine.[15] The westernmost of the three kingdoms formed the territorial basis of what later became France, and the easternmost, Germany.

If this interpretation of the Treaty of Verdun is correct, then the treaty is the first, and in some senses perhaps the only, example of international boundaries consciously being drawn in accordance with some set of geographical principles, as opposed to being drawn solely on the basis of military conquest or some form of compromise resulting from military conflict. In the rest of this section, I shall briefly examine other major events – notably the Congress of Vienna in 1814–15 and the Paris Peace Conference in 1919 – whose agendas were largely committed to the drawing of multiple international boundaries. The purpose of this discussion is to

determine the extent to which the outcomes of these meetings were based on the similar kind of reasoning that apparently determined the provisions of the Treaty of Verdun.

The interpretation of the treaty that I have presented has
been strongly contested by scholars who claim that the tri-
partite division of the Carolingian Empire was based on
much more pragmatic and political concerns than the forgo-
ing analysis suggests.[16] Whose interpretation is right is not
our concern. The point is that drawing boundaries for
princes and kings has rarely been carried out by experts according to any set of predetermined abstract principles. If,
however, we were ever deliberately to set out to draw the
boundaries of modern city-states, this is exactly what we
would have to do.

There are, of course, historical precedents for city-states.
They emerged in the Middle Ages and were eventually
snuffed out by the almost universal acceptance of the sovereign territorial state as the basic unit of government throughout the world. Quasi-independent cities such as San Marino
and Monaco are the direct descendants of city-states, while
others – Hamburg, Bremen, and Berlin in Germany, for example, and Basel and Geneva in Switzerland – have become
constituent units of federal states.[17] But most of the famous
city-states of northern Germany and Italy have become municipal units of government just like thousands of other city-
states around the world.

In some respects, city-states can be seen as a kind of mid-
way point between feudalism on the one hand and sovereign
territorial states on the other.[18] Feudalism involves intricate
webs of loyalties and allegiances, with no one institution having unfettered authority and where either precise territorial
boundaries do not exist at all or various authoritative figures

(e.g., bishops, dukes, kings, etc.) have overlapping authority in different territories. This is in contrast to the sovereign territorial state, which is characterized by precise boundaries and clear constitutional rules about who has the legal authority to do what within that territory. City-states had relatively well-defined boundaries and were recognized as sovereign entities in the Treaty of Westphalia in 1648. But they did not survive. Neither, of course, did feudalism. One of the central themes of this book is that a form of "democratized feudalism" is likely to be a more relevant model for the governance of our large cities than is the model of the territorial sovereign state. In any event, understanding why city-states of a few centuries ago gave way to sovereign territorial states might help us understand some of the weaknesses in current attempts to resurrect the city-state concept.

Hendrik Spruyt argues that, during the period from the eleventh to the fifteenth centuries, two distinct types of city-states emerged in Europe. In northern Germany dozens of independent city-states emerged after the German king (the Holy Roman emperor) surrendered control over towns and cities to feudal lords. Commercial elites in these various cities then banded together in leagues or confederations – most notably the Hanseatic League – to gain and maintain their autonomy from the feudal lords. In order to advance commerce, the merchants successfully promoted a legal system for trade that was enforced by the league. Nevertheless, within the Hanseatic League, Spruyt writes,

> [i]t is true that the individual towns maintained considerable autonomy and pursued their own specific interests. For example, some of the more important towns acquired considerable territories. This was partially due to deliberate

town policy. They strove to acquire territory with strategic value to control incursions by lords and to gain cheap supplies. This was partially due to investment by affluent merchants in the surrounding countryside. Thus Lübeck had about 240 villages and Hamburg almost 100 under their control.[19]

Because of their membership in leagues, city-states were not fully sovereign in the sense that the territorial states were. Because the leagues had no stable membership and hence no defined territory, they were not sovereign either. This form of accidental federalism – in contrast to the deliberate federal system designed by the American founding fathers – meant that the leagues and their constituent units ultimately could not participate in the emerging international system of sovereign states. As this latter system became increasingly important for trade and commerce and for issues of war and peace, the city-states ultimately could not avoid being formally absorbed into territorial sovereign states.

In contrast to city-states in northern Germany, those in northern Italy were characterized by an alliance between the bourgeoisie and the urban-based aristocracy that was aimed at collectively resisting outside dominance from both the pope and the Holy Roman emperor.[20] The rule of the Medicis in Florence was a prime example of such an arrangement. Much more so than the German city-states, the Italian ones sought to extend their territory, so much so that Venice, for example, annexed much of the Dalmatian coast. By 1450, Venice, Milan, and Florence had either absorbed or come to dominate most of the other city-states.[21] But the hinterlands of these city-states were not easily integrated. Towns that were absorbed by Italian city-states kept much of their independence because there was no organizing principle whereby they should follow central directives or policies.

Spruyt notes that "none of these [Italian] city-states developed formal kingship. Despots called themselves dukes or princes, but not kings, although they basically exercised regalian rights. The government of the city-state was always tied to some faction."[22] There were, in short, fundamental contradictions at the heart of the Italian city-states. For example, their political existence sprang from their urban roots, but much of their acquired territory had little or no historical connection to such roots. Unlike the relationship that developed between the king of France and the people within the territory of France, there was no institution that could serve to unite residents in the urban centre and the rural periphery within an expanding Italian city-state. France was much larger in territory than any of the Italian city-states, but paradoxically, France was much better equipped to nurture a coherent and united political community. As we shall see, this problem – the lack of a unifying interest between centre and periphery – still remains for the advocates of modern-day city-states. It is easy to see why an investment banker living in a Toronto waterfront condo would be loyal to a city-state of Toronto, but it is not so evident that the manager of an agricultural supply business in Brantford should experience similar political attachments. Is it not easier for both to feel a similar and common bond to much larger territorial units, such as Canada and Ontario?

From the emergence of sovereign territorial states until at least the end of the Second World War, boundaries of sovereign states have constantly been changing, usually as a result of war, hardly ever as part of any grand plan. There have been, however, two significant occasions during which

world leaders were charged with restructuring the boundaries of several sovereign states at the same time. The first
such occasion was the Congress of Vienna in 1814–15.

The most important objectives of the congress were to restore France to its pre-Napoleonic boundaries and to structure its eastern frontier such that any future expansionary
ambitions would be difficult to achieve.[23] To this end, the
Kingdom of the Netherlands (including what is now Belgium and Luxembourg) was established to the north; the
central Rhineland was placed under the control of Prussia
and other German states (notably Baden, Württemberg, and
Bavaria) that were all part of a renewed German Confederation; Switzerland was re-established as a neutral country
with modified boundaries that are still in place today; to the
south, the Kingdom of Piedmont-Sardinia was restored to
the House of Savoy, which later in the century became the
royal family of a united Italy; Austria was given control
over what is now the rest of northern Italy, including Venice
and its Dalmatian hinterland, and in the east, Russia was
given control over Finland and most of Poland.

The key point is that the series of territorial settlements
agreed to at the Congress of Vienna had almost nothing to
do with the idea of establishing the boundaries of sovereign
states in accordance with any set of common abstract principles. Participants in the congress deliberately set out to create a "balance of power" in Europe such that all the major
powers were well enough satisfied with what they got that
they would abstain in the future from wars of territorial
conquest. In this regard, the settlements were relatively successful. Until the outbreak of the First World War, interstate
warfare in Europe related mainly to the unification of Italy,
which involved a reduction in Austria's territory, and the

unification of Germany, in which the Franco-Prussian War of 1870–71 played a central role. That same war caused an adjustment in the boundary between France and Germany that remained in dispute until the end of the Second World War and the creation of what is now the European Union. The next major redrawing of European boundaries occurred at the Paris Peace Conference in 1919 following the First World War. President Woodrow Wilson had famously declared that the new boundaries should reflect the principle of national self-determination. Although groups of experts were assigned to determine the territories of various nations, their work was inconclusive and unimportant in determining the outcome of the negotiations. In late 1919, Wilson himself admitted to the United States Congress that when he originally presented his case for self-determination, it was "without knowledge that nationalities existed, which are coming to us day after day."[24] The Paris Peace Conference led to the recognition of the sovereign independence of Poland, Hungary, Czechoslovakia, Austria, Latvia, Lithuania, and Estonia, as well as to a substantial reduction in the territory of Germany and Russia (which had become the Soviet Union during the course of the war). Yugoslavia (as it was eventually named) emerged from the wreckage of the southernmost part of the former Austro-Hungarian Empire and from the previously independent states of Serbia and Montenegro. Although the Treaty of Versailles was clearly unsuccessful in maintaining the peace in Europe, the external boundaries of Hungary, the Czech Republic and Slovakia, Austria, Latvia, Lithuania, Estonia, Denmark, Belgium, and France remain today as they were established by the treaty or by processes deriving directly therefrom. Another country that was established in the aftermath of the First

World War was the Irish Free State (Eire), known as the Republic of Ireland since 1949. The partition of Ireland in 1920 has been seen as temporary by Irish nationalists, but the boundaries between the republic and Northern Ireland have never been altered.

Tony Judt has recently written that at "the conclusion of the First World War it was borders that were invented and adjusted, while people were on the whole left in place. After 1945 what happened was rather the opposite: with one major exception boundaries stayed broadly intact and people were moved instead."[25] The major exception was Poland. Its north-south boundaries were moved to the west so as to reduce the territory of Germany and enlarge that of the Soviet Union. The enlargement included the absorption of the three Baltic republics, but following the collapse of the Soviet Union in 1989, they were to re-emerge with their original boundaries intact. The most significant boundary problem of the postwar period has been that between Israel and Palestine, a problem that has still to be resolved. All we can say at this point is that, efforts of the United Nations notwithstanding, the boundaries of Israel have been determined more by the successes of Zionist and Israeli armed forces than by any other relevant factor.

As far as sovereign states are concerned, the most significant postwar development has been the accession to sovereignty of virtually all of the territories in the world that had once been European colonies. Many such colonies had been originally assigned to their respective colonial powers by either the Congress of Vienna or the Paris Peace Conference. As has been frequently observed, the leaders of independence movements in the various colonies were almost always content to accept existing colonial boundaries so as to prevent violent conflicts relating to new ones. Hence we have dozens of boundary lines around the world, especially in Africa, that were hastily drawn for the purposes of colonial administration in the nineteenth century and are now uncontested among sovereign states.[26]

The bloody breakup of British India into India and Pakistan and then the secession of Bangladesh from Pakistan are the most notable exceptions that prove the rule. The boundary between India and Pakistan is still not settled, with the armistice line going right through a territory (Kashmir) that had been under the control of a Hindu maharajah prior to independence. A rare example of colonial boundaries being peacefully changed can be found in what is now Cameroon in west Africa. The colony was originally German but was taken over by a joint Anglo-French force in 1916, leading to the creation of British Cameroons and French Cameroons under mandates from the League of Nations and then the United Nations. French Cameroons gained independence as the Republic of Cameroon in 1960. In 1961 the United Nations (UN) conducted plebiscites in each of the northern and southern zones of British Cameroons. People in the north voted to join Nigeria, and those in the south voted to join Cameroon, creating the second country in the world with French and English as the two official languages. The history of the emergence of Cameroon with its current boundaries is recounted here only because such a history is so unusual among the sovereign states that have emerged from colonialism since 1945. A much less peaceful African boundary change occurred in 1993 when Eritrea seceded from Ethiopia, the only secession that has ever occurred among sovereign African nations.[27] Attempted secessions from the Congo (Katanga) and Nigeria (Biafra) were stopped by civil wars.[28]

Rhetoric about constant change in the world is sometimes fuelled by reference to the breakup of the Soviet Union, Yugoslavia, and Czechoslovakia. The coming apart of sovereign states is indeed a significant development, especially for Canadians. But, from the perspective of boundary watchers, surely the most significant fact about these breakups is that, in the final analysis, the boundaries of the new sovereign states that have emerged all correspond exactly to. sub-national boundaries drawn many years ago.[29] In what was the Soviet Union, they were the boundaries of the "Soviet Socialist Republics" that made up the "Union." In Yugoslavia they were the boundaries of the six constituent republics. The emergence of Kosovo as an independent state in 2008 is somewhat different because Kosovo had existed only as an "autonomous province" within Serbia since 1974, and even this status was effectively lost in 1990 when Yugoslav president Slobodan Miloševic closed down its elected assembly. Kosovo's very existence, let alone its boundaries, are disputed by Serbia, but the boundaries that are claimed by the newly independent state are those of the former autonomous province. While the Soviet and Yugoslav breakups were accompanied by considerable political tension and violence, the breakup of Czechoslovakia in 1993 was completely peaceful. The boundary between the new sovereign states of the Czech Republic and Slovakia was not an issue. It corresponded without question to the boundary originally drawn in the nineteenth century to separate two administrative divisions within the Austro-Hungarian Empire.

Peter J. Taylor, a geographer, has written about the recent stability of international borders. He claims that respect for international borders since 1945 has produced "a mummified world political map." He also notes that in "Europe the solidification of the post-war settlement was achieved at Helsinki in 1975, so that for the first time in the history of the world no state formally claimed the territory of another in continental Europe."[30] He further bolsters his case by pointing to the world's response to Iraq's invasion of Kuwait in 1990 and to the fact that aggressive neighbours did not move in to take over from failed states such as Liberia and Somalia. But Taylor draws different conclusions from this analysis than I do. He assumes, unlike Spruyt, that city-states lost their autonomy because they needed the military security provided by a large territorial state. He writes:

[I]f state territories are now guaranteed ... this means effectively that the original security function of the state is seriously eroded. Coercion may be required internally but the problem of outside aggressors is lessening. However, city states were always able to deal with internal dissent, they only lost their political power to territorial states because of outside threats. Hence we can say that objectively we are reaching a situation where city states can again prosper in the world-system ... Singapore is perhaps the model for the future, organizing South-east Asia but without the military, economic, and social costs of being part of a dominant territorial state in the region. Which leads us to ask whether London as world city needs Britain, or New York as world city requires to be part of a large territorial state that is the USA.[31]

Writing in 1995, Taylor can hardly be criticized for failing to anticipate the terrorist attack on New York's Twin Towers and the resulting increased reliance by New Yorkers on the security apparatus of the United States.[32] But – especially as a geographer – he can be criticized for failing to note the potential difficulties in drawing boundaries around the potential city-states of London and New York. Like Singapore, Manhattan is an island, but Taylor was clearly not referring to a city-state of Manhattan. In any event, Singapore's ethnic makeup (primarily Chinese) is significantly different from that on the Malay mainland. This is what caused Singapore to become an independent city-state, not some abstract desire to replicate in southeast Asia the old model of European city-states.

Drawing boundaries around a sovereign area for New York or London would be no easy task, and I will take up an exploration of the relevant problems in the rest of this book. Before leaving the subject of the boundaries of sovereign states, however, we must remember that sovereign states are the territorial vessels in which most of our political life is contained. Although there is much political theory and philosophy relating to almost all aspects of political life, Allen Buchanan reminds us that "liberal political theory has remarkably little to say about the ethics of creating and changing boundaries."[33] In most parts of the world they are simply accepted as political facts of life. Buchanan goes on to state that political theorists have had even less to say about intra-state boundaries,[34] to which we turn our attention in the next section of this chapter and for the rest of the book.

INTRA-STATE BOUNDARIES

In federations such as Canada, the United States, Germany, Switzerland, Belgium, and Spain, the responsibility for local government rests with the constituent parts of the federation. Thus, we need to know about the intra-state boundaries that surround them, just as we need to know about the boundaries of sovereign states. Not surprisingly, my main point in relation to such boundaries is that they are generally as stable as those of sovereign states. They have emerged and stabilized in the same kind of unplanned way that the boundaries of sovereign states have. However, there is one significant example among non-federal sovereign states in which an attempt was made to divide the state into regions whose boundaries were determined according to set of predetermined, rational criteria. The example is France, and it merits our attention.

[margin handwriting: stability of sub-national jurisdictions]

Prior to the French Revolution, France, like most other European countries, contained a bewildering array of overlapping subdivisions, many dating back to feudal times, others created to meet a particular objective of the administrators of the central state. Throughout the eighteenth century, various plans were presented to clear up the confusion. The early ones were generally aimed at dividing France into a relatively small number of units. One was designed to create twenty units "as equal in wealth as possible."[35] Other plans suggested many more units. In 1780, the king's topographer devised a scheme in which the country was divided roughly into nine squares, and each one of these into nine more, producing a total of eighty-one. The Marquis de Condorcet, the well-known mathematician and philosopher, conceived of a different system of districts, each of which combined communities that lay within a day's travel of one another.[36] After the revolution, the Constituent Assembly, in its desire to wipe out France's royalist past, took such schemes very seriously indeed. In January 1790, the assembly voted for a plan that was remarkably similar to that of the king's topographer, although it did take account of local topography and some traditional boundaries. France was divided into eighty-three *départements*, two of which were territorially small – one for Paris and another for Corsica.[37] The number was adjusted as France's external territories ebbed and flowed, but there was a net increase of six between 1790 and 1968, including a permanent increase of three in 1860 when France was ceded Savoy and Nice by King Victor Emmanuel of Savoy prior to his becoming king of Italy. Six more have been added since 1968 (not counting overseas *départements*) as a result of reorganizations in the Paris area and in Corsica.

Since 1790, the French *départements* have proven a remarkably stable unit of sub-national government.[38] Despite Edmund Burke's rants about the barbarity of the French revolutionaries in wiping out all the vestiges of traditional territorial boundaries in France, the *départements* have generally survived, in recent years at least, with far less territorial disruption than have the counties in non-revolutionary England. While their role within the governmental system of France has changed dramatically over the decades and centuries, they remain as the basic building blocks of French territorial administration. Most have existed with unchanged boundaries since long before most of the constituent parts of the American and Canadian federations were created.

Although both the United States and Canada have admitted new units to their federations as recently as 1959 (Alaska and Hawaii) and 1949 (Newfoundland) respectively, there have been scarcely any changes in boundaries of any such units in either country. In the United States, the last time such a change took place was in 1863, during the American Civil War, when West Virginia seceded from Virginia. Most of the western states that joined the union in the late nineteenth and early twentieth centuries had been organized as federal territories decades before. Their state boundaries are the same as the territorial ones. The only exceptions are North Dakota and South Dakota, which became states in 1896 when the Dakota Territory was split into two. In 1977, the State of Nevada took legal action for the "return" of 350 square miles of territory that had been inaccurately surveyed in 1872. *The Historical Atlas of the United States* notes that "[t]he case was settled as most 20th Century border disputes are: in favor of the occupants."[39] Despite the fact that state boundaries bisect (or trisect in the case of New York) dozens of densely populated metropolitan areas (e.g., Philadelphia, St Louis, Cincinnati, Kansas City), proposals for redrawing state boundaries in the United States are simply not on any mainstream political agenda.

Prior to the amalgamation in 1896 that created today's boundaries for New York City, there were proposals that Manhattan become its own state.[40] More recently, as part of a plan to spur economic growth in upstate New York, a think tank affiliated with the Business Council of New York State explored ways of granting more political autonomy to the upstate area. Here is an excerpt from its analysis: "Politics and costs are imposed on the Upstate economy in ways that would not happen if Upstate were a standalone state on its own ... We hesitate to raise the issue, lest we set off a pointless discussion about whether Upstate should be its own state. Secession would be impossible ... But given the prolonged lag in Upstate's economy, it is time to think seriously about whether there is a way of restructuring the relationship to give Upstate the opportunity – indeed the freedom – to reduce some of its disadvantages."[41] Significantly, the analysis does not address boundaries, even for a form of restructuring well short of secession. All the comparisons of economic data are between New York City and the six largest upstate metropolitan areas.

Canada is no different. The last time provincial boundaries were changed was in 1912, when the boundaries of Manitoba, Ontario, and Quebec were all extended northward to take in parts of the Northwest Territories.[42] Although Canada has experienced just about every conceivable kind of constitutional debate and proposal in the last few decades, there has been no discussion about redrawing provincial boundaries. Occasionally there is talk of "Maritime Union," but even this radical proposal does not question the boundary between New Brunswick and Quebec.[43] Indeed, one of the most notable features of the long-standing debate about possible Quebec independence is the general acknowledgment by all parties that, if Quebec ever separates, it will maintain its current boundaries, including the Quebec-Labrador boundary (in an uninhabited area) that was determined by the Judicial Committee of the Privy Council in 1927 and has never been officially accepted by the Quebec provincial government. Negotiations about changing Quebec boundaries in the event of independence are practically unthinkable.[44]

Herbert Emery, an economist at the University of Calgary, has been involved in various studies relating to provincial boundaries, the most serious being one for which he produced a "Commentary," co-authored by Ronald Kneebone and published by the C.D. Howe Institute in 2003, which asked *Should Alberta and Saskatchewan Unite?* Its conclusion about the prospects for union is highly skeptical: "In our view the fact that the fiscal regimes and the industrial policies of the two provinces have remained different over many years, suggests that these differences in preferences are firmly held."[45] In another study, Emery looks at the case for detaching northwestern Ontario (including Thunder Bay) and adding it to Manitoba. Once again, he arrives at a similar conclusion: "While there is no overwhelming case against new institutional options, there does not appear at this time to be an overwhelming case for them either."[46] Boundaries of constituent units within other federations have also been remarkably stable. The most notable exception has been the secession in 1979 of northern Jura from the canton of Berne in Switzerland following a local referendum in 1974 and a national one in 1978. Jura was the first new canton in Switzerland since 1815. Theories explaining the secession are complex, involving a mixture of linguistic, religious, economic, and geographical considerations. Malcolm Anderson concludes: "No criteria for settling the rival claims of these theories exist and all rest on unreliable data."[47]

Unlike other federations, the Federal Republic of Germany contains a provision (Article 29) that outlines a procedure for redrawing the boundaries of the constituent units (*Länder*) "in order to guarantee that they have the size and capacity to carry out their tasks effectively."[48] The provision dates back to the foundation of the republic in 1949, when it was assumed that the sometimes hastily drawn original boundaries created under the auspices of the three Western occupying forces would need to be revisited after the new republic was fully operational. In 1952, three *Länder* were merged to create Baden-Württemberg, but there have been no further changes in any of the western *Land* boundaries despite numerous reports and proposals advocating change. One participant in the process refers to the "sport of map drawing" and states that "[t]oo often the results are poorly substantiated products of fantasy."[49] In 1989, five new *Länder* were added as a result of the dissolution of the German Democratic Republic (GDR). Their boundaries were almost identical to the boundaries of the five *Länder* that had been created in the Soviet zone of occupation immediately after the end of the Second World War but had been abolished by the GDR in 1952.[50] The federal systems of Belgium and Spain are of much more recent origin. Spain became a federation with the adoption of its 1978 constitution, which provided for seventeen "autonomous communities" as the constituent units. The federal system has emerged as asymmetrical because the "historic nationalities" of the Basque Country, Catalonia, and Galicia have taken on more powers from the Spanish state than have the other autonomous communities.[51] The drawing of the boundaries for these three areas appears not to have been difficult, as they have been generally accepted over a long period of time. The boundaries of the other autonomous communities were also based on long-standing historical divisions (including the ancient kingdom of Navarre) or groups of administrative regions (provinces) of the Spanish state. The only autonomous community whose boundaries appear genuinely new are those of Madrid. The boundaries of the Spanish capital *do* serve extremely well as the boundaries of a city-state within a federation – and we shall return to consider them in later chapters.

Belgium became a federation in 1989. Two of its territorial units – Flanders and Wallonia – represent the historic territorial bases of Belgium's two long-standing linguistic communities.[52] The third territory is Brussels, a bilingual urban enclave within Flanders. Agreeing on the boundaries of Brussels was politically difficult, but the issues involved had very little to do with effective urban governance.

As indicated earlier, a few of the constituent units of the German and Swiss federations have long histories as city-states, and Madrid and Brussels have more recently obtained

such a status. Advocates of a city-state for Toronto would be
thrilled if their city had a similar provincial status within the
Canadian federation, but before this idea can be taken seriously, it is important to know more about these existing cases
of city-states within federations. We shall examine these examples in more detail in chapter 4.

CONCLUSION

Boundaries of nation-states have historically changed as a result of war. Even in the United States, the only case in which
secession has taken place within an existing state was during
the American Civil War. It is true that, since about 1960, the
breakup of colonial empires and the dissolution of the Soviet
Union and Yugoslavia have led to many more sovereign
states in the world, but the boundaries of almost all of the
new countries replicate the imperial or sub-national boundaries that were already in place. Creating new boundaries for
national entities is a politically perilous undertaking, and
most politicians try to avoid it whenever they possibly can.

Unlikelyhood of new boundaries about the municipal level (and even then) — deference to stability.

3

Boundaries for Municipal Corporations

The original idea behind municipal corporations was that they would have territorial jurisdiction within the built-up areas of cities. When cities had walls, the walls themselves often constituted the original boundaries. When the city grew beyond the walls, its boundaries were usually extended. In the well-known case of the Corporation of the City of London, however, the boundary expansions stopped in the Middle Ages after the city had expanded into a few areas known as "bars" (e.g., Temple Bar) just outside the walls. Even today, the City of London covers only 2.6 square kilometres (approximately one square mile) and has a population of only about 7,500. The corporate boundaries of most cities in the Western world have expanded much more than those of London, but few have kept up completely with outward urban expansion. The main argument of this book is that it is now impossible even to define the outer limits of urban expansion. To the extent that the boundaries have not expanded, they increasingly take on the apparently arbitrary characteristics that we often associate with the boundaries of sovereign states.

DO CITIES NEED BOUNDARIES?

The kind of analysis of nation-states undertaken by Alesina and Spolaore forces us to consider whether cities need boundaries at all.[1] If a city exists within a state or within a decentralized unit within a state, why does the city itself need a formal, multi-functional unit of government? Perhaps the functions of government not included within the jurisdiction of the state itself or of its decentralized units could be handled by a "maze" of special-purpose authorities, each with own appropriate territory.[2] Co-ordination and control could be handled by the relevant central government (the provincial government in Canada's case). In this arrangement, there would be no municipalities, no city governments. Hence there would be no need for city boundaries. It is important to note that this is *not* a centralized system without local government. There would be many local governments, each with its own function. Each could be controlled by locally elected citizens (as school boards are in most North American cities). What would be missing would be a multi-functional local government.

From the perspective of the city dwellers, the success of such a system would depend on such factors as the extent to which the single-purpose authorities had access to sufficient resources to carry out their responsibilities; the ability of voters to track the activities of a considerable number of such authorities; and the capacity of the central governments to co-ordinate the activities of the authorities in such a way as to be sensitive to overall city needs and preferences. This last factor would likely be dependent on the political strength of city residents within the central government. If they formed the majority of the jurisdiction's voters, chances for a responsive

for local growth, held in
political champion, for political
champions, need defined area to
champion

central government would be high; if their city were just one
of many cities and small towns, then their particular city
would likely not get much attention and its various special-
purpose authorities could well act against each other in counterproductive ways.

But in the real world of democratic politics, it is hard to
imagine how a city could thrive without some kind of elected
champion with electoral legitimacy to speak on behalf of at
least the residents of the central area. Such legitimacy would
be unlikely to derive from any election for a special-purpose
authority, no matter how important its single function might
be. In short, a city needs a mayor, not necessarily for functional reasons, but definitely for political reasons, the kinds
of reasons that are not analysed in the work of Alesina and
Spolaore. But even a mayor and a city government with limited functional responsibilities need a defined territory, if for
no other reason than to determine who is eligible to vote in
mayoral elections. Determining such boundaries (or providing a mechanism for their determination) is usually a responsibility of the central government.

In the spirit of the kind of analysis of the size of nations that
Alesina and Spolaore provided, it is interesting to think about
what might happen if there were no central-government involvement and if the mayor and city government had no
functional responsibilities other than to speak on behalf of
the area for which they were elected. We can assume for this
function, as Alesina and Spolaore do for all functions, that
there are infinite economies of scale and voters have an opportunity to choose borders. In such circumstances, we
can hypothesize an outcome similar to what Alesina and
Spolaore conclude about the size of nations: the city borders
would expand until the area became so heterogeneous in

preferences about city life that it would be difficult for voters to agree on anything significant for the mayor to say on their behalf. Another, more political way of stating this is that city boundaries in these circumstances should be drawn in such a way as to encapsulate a community of people who share similar basic values about what they want in city life. This is probably a very good way to think about city boundaries, but it is not the way that has been predominant within central governments, outside the United States at least.

EXPANDING MUNICIPAL BOUNDARIES

More than any other part of this book, the remaining sections of this chapter are explicitly concerned with municipal boundaries. In particular, they focus on relationships within particular city-regions between the central-city municipality and its municipal neighbours, which are sometimes rural and more often suburban. In this context, I shall be using the term "city" to refer to the central-city municipality rather than to the city-region as a whole.

What has stopped the outward expansion of city municipal boundaries? Much of the answer depends on the particular municipal legislation that applies in the various jurisdictions. However, the following account holds true for many jurisdictions, especially for those whose their historical roots are in England. Let us assume that sometime in the past an area of urban settlement is officially designated by the central government as a "city" and that it is surrounded by a rural area with its own arrangements for local governance, originally feudal and later municipal. A council is chosen or elected within the city to oversee the provision of local public services. The city boundaries include all the territory containing relatively dense (non-rural) residential settlement and all the factories, shops, and offices in which the residents of the town are employed. Because the boundary drawers are far-sighted, they even include within the city some vacant land to accommodate future urban growth. Let us also assume that city residents are generally successful in their economic endeavours. Businesses grow and more people move to the city because employment opportunities are abundant and the council has helped ensure that it is a pleasant place to live.

Sooner or later, though, the city will have to face the problem of no more available land for new development. There are three possible consequences. The first is the most unlikely. It might be that new development simply cannot happen because urban development in the rural areas is not allowed and city residents must accept a halt to growth (the value of their own property, at least for the short-term, will rise because they possess a scarce commodity, urban land).

The second possible consequence – much more likely – is that the authorities in the surrounding rural area are willing and able to approve urban growth, though without a change in boundaries. Depending on the arrangements for the financing of municipal services, such a policy might have the effect of lowering taxation levels for current rural residents, because the resulting population growth in the rural area means that there are now more people with whom to share costs. Rural residents who own property near the city would be especially fortunate because their property values would inevitably increase as their land changes from rural to urban/industrial use. Even the new urban-minded residents in the rural municipality might consider themselves better off than if they had located in the city. They might be able to escape paying for the very facilities and services (i.e., the ones located in the adjacent urban centre) that were a factor in attracting them to the area. This second possibility contains the seeds of many of the issues at the heart of political disputes between cities and their suburbs.

The third possible consequence is that the boundaries of the city would be extended so as to accommodate the new growth. This process of boundary extension is known as "annexation." Municipal annexation is rarely easy, but it is less difficult when the land in question is rural rather than fully developed. Since the most obvious purpose of annexation is to allow for a single urban municipality to provide for orderly outward urban expansion, it makes sense that annexation should, at least ideally, occur prior to development rather than after.

If annexation is to be allowed at all, central governments must provide a procedure for it. Such a procedure might of necessity involve some form of local negotiation and agreement. The agreement could involve only the two relevant authorities, or there might be a requirement for approval by various local referendums, especially involving those residents and property owners most directly affected by the proposed change. The problem with requiring local agreement is that there is rarely any incentive for the municipality that is losing land to agree. Compensation payments, however, can sometimes be used to purchase agreement. The position adopted by landowners in the affected area usually depends on whether or not annexation will increase the value of their land. If development is only possible if the land is within the boundaries of the central urban municipality, then they will likely be in favour. If development is possible whatever the outcome of the annexation dispute, then their position will depend on taxation levels and particular local political circumstances.

As an alternative to obtaining local agreement, the central government might allow annexation issues to be settled by the courts – that is, by some form of administrative or quasi-judicial tribunal or by some special authority created only to deal with municipal boundary disputes. The problems here are predictable. Such a process can be very expensive, especially when highly paid lawyers and experts become involved in public hearings. Sometimes, however, the issues at stake are fundamentally political rather than technical, and it is simply inappropriate in a democracy for unelected people (such as those appointed to sit on tribunals) to make such decisions about the political futures of significant urban areas. This last problem can always be overcome by ensuring that the process allows a relevant minister in the central government to over-rule the tribunal's decisions. Such a provision can make life politically difficult for a minister, as he or she will be pressured to overrule various controversial decisions. But coping with such difficulties – and being accountable for their resolution – is exactly what central-government ministers are paid to do.

As long as municipalities are not constitutionally protected against changes being made in their boundaries without their consent, central governments can always use their legislative authority to sort out boundary disputes. The main difficulty is that most of the members of any central legislature will almost by definition have no interest in a local issue that does not affect their own constituencies. At best, such legislation is a waste of their time; at worst, it is an opportunity for them to extract favours from one side or another in return for their vote. Only when the resolution of a boundary dispute creates significant precedents or when it affects the future of the largest cities would such an issue seem appropriate for legislative settlement.

Regardless of how they are brought about, annexations, while solving some problems, can create new ones of their own. For example, even if everyone accepts in principle the need for an annexation, there can be serious disagreements about its size. Should there periodically be huge annexations or is it better to take in a few hectares on a regular basis? Sometimes the threat of an unwanted annexation provokes residents or landowners in a rural area to try to establish a new urban municipality within the disputed territory, the belief being that it will be more difficult (legally or politically) for an entire urban municipality to be annexed than for part of a rural one. Whether or not this calculation is correct, and whether or not such new incorporations are possible, depends greatly on the particular legal regime established by the central government. In the United States, the calculation has generally been correct and the incorporation of new municipalities is relatively easy. This helps explain why many large American metropolitan areas contain dozens, if not hundreds, of distinct urban municipalities.[3]

Another problem with annexation arises when two urban municipalities that are near one another each absorb so much previously rural land around their original boundaries that they eventually become contiguous jurisdictions, each responsible for part of what has become a single urban area. In such circumstances, one fact is clear: further annexation along the two municipalities' common boundary is difficult, if not pointless. Indeed, for many people – whom we can label as "consolidationists" – it is the boundary itself that has become the problem.

This discussion has shown how urban areas can evolve in such a way that they contain many separate municipalities. Adjoining rural municipalities might have become urban

What about non-adjacent rural areas?

over time; new urban municipalities might have been established within a former part of a rural municipality; two previously distinct urban areas might have grown into each
other; or all or some of these processes might have occurred
simultaneously. Ever since the mid-nineteenth century, consolidationists – politicians, civil servants, academics, and
sometimes even real-estate developers – have observed
such phenomena with growing concern. They refer to the
tendency for increasing number of municipalities within a
single urban area as "fragmentation," and they have
worked hard to reverse the trend.

The consolidationists won their greatest victory more than a
hundred years ago, in 1898, when the legislature of New York
State merged New York (Manhattan), Brooklyn, Richmond,
the Bronx, and Staten Island to form a new City of New York.[4]
Although the New York area could be considered consolidated a hundred years ago, it scarcely can be now. The City of
New York now includes only 7.3 million of the 18.3 million
people that the American federal Bureau of Statistics considers
to be part of what it calls the Metropolitan Statistical Area of
New York–Northern New Jersey–Long Island. The municipal
boundaries of the city have not changed since 1898, but
growth continues all around it.

One of the consolidationists' main difficulties has been
finding agreement on appropriate boundaries. For some purposes, such as regional planning, boundaries should probably extend quite far out into the countryside, especially if
there is continuing pressure to allow people who work in the
city to live and build wherever they wish to in the countryside.[5] But for other purposes, boundaries such as these might
take in too much. For example, the objective of efficiency in
service delivery is compromised if such services as garbage

collection and public transit are extended into sparsely populated areas where unit costs are high. Similarly, equity concerns arise if farmers are forced to pay for city services they rarely use.

TWO-TIER METROPOLITAN GOVERNMENTS

In response to such problems, consolidationists have long proposed a two-tier system of urban (or metropolitan) government. For many consolidationists, such a system is superior to complete consolidation, especially for very large urban areas. A two-tier system of municipal government is one in which one municipal council is established to cover the entire urban area, while local councils are retained to manage those municipal functions that seem more local in scope. In short, a two-tier system of municipal government is like a municipal federation, with the central government determining the nature of the federal constitution or at least acting as a referee between the two levels.

London and Toronto have been the best-known examples of the urban two-tier local-government system. Although the upper-tier London County Council (LCC) was established in 1888, the twenty-eight relatively weak lower-tier "metropolitan boroughs" were not organized until ten years later. The creation of the metropolitan boroughs did not affect the continued existence (with the same boundaries)of the Corporation of the City of London. In 1965, the British parliament abolished the LCC and replaced it with the Greater London Council (GLC). The GLC – comprising thirty-two "Greater London boroughs" that were functionally stronger than their lower-tier predecessors in the LCC – covered a much wider territory. The GLC was itself abolished in 1986 when Margaret

Thatcher was prime minister. More recently, the Labour prime minister Tony Blair established a new upper-tier council for metropolitan London. The council is supposed to be responsible for strategic infrastructure decisions for the London area. More importantly, for the first time ever, the wider London area now has its own powerful political spokesperson: a directly elected mayor.[6] Confusingly, however, the Lord Mayor of the old City of London continues to travel around the world representing the interests of London's financial services industries, which are still headquartered in "the City."

Toronto's upper-tier local government, the Municipality of Metropolitan Toronto (Metro) came into being in 1954, bringing together thirteen different municipalities. These were consolidated into six in 1966. However, in 1998, Metro and its six constituent units were all merged into the new city of Toronto.[7] Experience in London and Toronto indicates that two-tier metropolitan government is at best controversial, at worst unstable. Similarly chequered histories are available for Rotterdam, Copenhagen, Barcelona,[8] and Winnipeg.[9]

Two-tier systems only partially solve boundary problems. Few people are ever satisfied with the upper-tier boundary. Land-use planners usually find the territory too small, while rural or outer-suburban residents have difficulty understanding why they must be included if they rarely go near the city centre. The lower-tier boundaries can also cause difficulties, especially if the representational system at the upper tier treats all lower-tier units with a degree of equality, entitling each of them to the same number of representatives on the council regardless of their population. But the greatest problem is that, even though the upper tier provides at least a partial antidote to geographical fragmentation, its very creation has bifurcated the activities of existing municipal governments. Areas previously served by one municipal government are now served by two. The coordination of their activities within dense urban settlements is possible, but not easy.

The advantages and disadvantages of two-tier systems of urban government are well known to anyone familiar with the operations of the two tiers of government within federal systems. Now they are becoming familiar to residents of unitary states of the European Union. City residents in many European countries now have to contend with four or five distinct tiers of government, each with its own range of assigned functions. Even if, within Europe, existing states were somehow to give way to city-states, the new city-states (whatever their boundaries) would be less than sovereign because so many important government functions would presumably remain as the ongoing responsibilities of the European Union. Indeed, it is commonly claimed that the very existence of the EU encourages Europeans to imagine new ways of structuring territorial governance, ways that inevitably involve a further diminution in the role of nation-states.[10]

LOCAL APPROVAL
FOR BOUNDARY CHANGES

As far as cities are concerned, it is quite impossible to generalize about their municipal boundaries. It is commonly observed almost everywhere that such boundaries are "artificial," having little or no connection with the territorial realities of urban life. There is always pressure from somewhere to eliminate these boundaries by merging urban municipalities. But, as we have seen, problems solved for some services by mergers create new problems for others. In any event, in most parts of the democratic world, the imposition of municipal mergers without local consent is increasingly rare. In the United States, the "home rule" provisions of many state constitutions prevent state legislatures from merging municipalities without local consent. In Europe, Article 5 of the European Charter of Local Self-Government adopted by the Council of Europe in 1985 state: "Changes in local authority boundaries shall not be made without prior consultation of the local communities concerned, possibly by means of a referendum where this is permitted by statute."

Local referendum results favourable to municipal mergers are equally rare. In the United States, considerable attention has been paid in some places to proposals for "city-county consolidation." In 2003, such a consolidation was approved by voters and implemented in Louisville, Kentucky.[11] In most American states, including Kentucky, counties cover the entire state and are responsible for a limited set of local public services, such as land registration and the legal recording of births and deaths. Municipalities are incorporated within counties so as to provide a wider range of services, especially in urban areas. Areas that are not incorporated are considered as "unincorporated" areas. In some counties, unincorporated areas receive a wide range of county-provided services, including policing by the county sheriff. Nevertheless, these areas are always subject to potential new municipal incorporations and/or annexation by existing municipalities within the county. Needless to say, it often takes complex political manoeuvring to determine the fate of unincorporated land that is sought by different institutional bidders.

A city-county consolidation is a merger of the largest city in the county with all of the unincorporated areas of its county. In the case of Louisville, the city merged with the unincorporated areas of Jefferson County after voters in both areas approved the proposal by referendum. Twenty-two incorporated suburban municipalities within the county were left untouched. Despite this "consolidation," no one can reasonably claim that the municipal boundaries have been simplified. The total number of incorporated municipalities remains the same; a large number of incorporated enclaves have been created; and the only thing that has changed is that there are no longer any unincorporated areas within the county. With its twenty-two suburban enclaves, Louisville is no closer to having appropriate boundaries for a potential city-state than it had before the consolidation. In any event, the built-up area extends considerably beyond Jefferson County.

METROPOLITAN AREAS
AS STATISTICAL ARTEFACTS

Everyone recognizes that urban areas are seldom contained within the boundaries of a single municipality. For all kinds of reasons, however, we have a greater need for statistical information relating to continuously built-up urban areas than for information relating to particular municipalities. This is why government agencies responsible for statistics in most developed countries collect information relating to "metropolitan areas." Defining the territorial boundaries of these metropolitan areas is in fact a crucially important way of defining the boundaries of our city-regions, even if these boundaries have no legal significance. We have already seen that the American legal scholar Gerald Frug would use the boundaries for American metropolitan areas as the territorial bases for his proposed regional assemblies.[12]

In many countries, it appears that national statistical agencies simply report data relating to sub-national boundaries that are created for the purposes of the national government and/or data relating to the territories of local government. In England, for example, the Office for National Statistics reports that the population of Greater London as determined by the 2001 census was 7,172,091. This is the territory covered by the Greater London Authority, which comprises the City of London and thirty-two London boroughs. Most observers of the London region, however, recognize that "the effective London economic region is ... larger even than the administrative boundary of the Greater London Authority ... It is in fact the 'Greater South East,'"[13] an area first described by Sir Peter Hall in 1989. The area contains over 12 million people, about 40 per cent of the population of England and Wales. But there are no official government statistics for the Greater South East.[14]

In North America, federal statistical agencies have developed elaborate procedures for determining the boundaries of, in Canada, census metropolitan areas (CMAS) and, in the United States, Metropolitan Statistical Areas (MSAS). A CMA in Canada must have an "urban area" of at least 50,000 people with a population density of 400 people per square kilometre. Any municipality having territory within this area – and any other municipalities that might be surrounded by these municipalities – form the "urban core." Other municipalities are added depending on complex calculations relating to commuting patterns as determined at the previous decennial census. For such an area to be designated as a CMA, it must have a total population of at least 100,000.[15] Once an area becomes a CMA, it remains one. This means that there are now two CMAS (Hamilton and Oshawa) that are contiguous with the Toronto CMA, as well as a third, St Catharines–Niagara, that adjoins Hamilton. Regardless of how integrated these CMAS become, Statistics Canada has no mechanism for consolidating them. In 2001, for the first time, the agency presented data in "thematic maps" for what it calls "The Extended Golden Horseshoe," an area including all of the four CMAS and considerable other territory as well. It presented similar data for extended areas around Montreal and Vancouver, as well as for the "Calgary-Edmonton Corridor." It is not yet clear whether such reporting will become a permanent feature of the Canadian census or if the means of determining the respective territories of such areas will be the subject of a public and consistent set of rules, as with the CMAS.

The American definition of an MSA is similar, but not identical, to that of the Canadian CMA. The main difference for our purposes between CMAS and MSAS is that the latter are allowed to merge with each other as they become more integrated. The original MSAS, however, retain their identities as "metropolitan divisions." Thus, the most populous MSA in the country – New York–Northern New Jersey–Long Island – comprises four separate metropolitan divisions, two of which each straddle the boundaries of two states (New York and New Jersey; New Jersey and Pennsylvania). The total population of this MSA, according to the 2000 census, was 18,323,002.[16]

After consultation with interested parties, the Office of Management and Budget (OMB) changed some of the various classifications of MSAS prior to the release of the 2000 census data. The consultative process indicated the perceived importance of MSA and related census classifications to the administration of various government programs.[17] As a result, the

OMB emphasizes, the classification system "does not equate to an urban-rural classification." It goes on:

> [The] OMB cautions that Metropolitan Statistical Area ... definitions should not be used to develop and implement Federal, state, and local nonstatistical programs and policies without full consideration of the effects of using these definitions for such purposes. These areas are not intended to serve as a general purpose geographic framework for nonstatistical activities, and they may or may not be suitable for use in program funding formulas.[18]

This statement is very important in relation to Gerald Frug's call for the creation of "regional assemblies" in the United States.[19] Although Frug pays little attention to the possible boundaries of such regions, he does suggest that the boundaries of MSAs might be appropriate. The OMB warns against using these boundaries to distribute government resources, but Frug wants to use them to determine a system for allocating resources. Frug is looking for a nonpolitical boundary. The OMB tries to develop such boundaries for statistical purposes, but its own consultative processes and its own warnings indicate that its rules for drawing MSA boundaries would be very problematic if the political and governmental uses of such boundaries were to become much greater than they already are.

There appear not to have been any public controversies in Canada about CMA boundaries and only one significant case in which these boundaries have been the basis for the deliberate creation of a governmental agency. In 1993, the Task Force on Greater Montreal, established by the Quebec government, recommended that a new level of metropolitan government be created for the Montreal area. It urged that the new Montreal Metropolitan Region comprise all of the 102 municipalities contained in the Montreal CMA at that time. To justify its proposal, the task force stated that the outer boundary of the CMA "best defines the socio-economic realities of the Montreal Metropolitan region ... The intensity of exchanges between municipalities located in this almost continuous urbanized space and the close daily interdependencies between the metropolitan markets of employment, production, consumption, and entertainment, constitute socio-economic realities which cross municipal borders to form a collective territory whose parts cannot be dissociated."[20]

Six years later, in 1999, the National Commission on Local Finances and Taxation in Quebec (the Bédard Commission) made a similar recommendation, except that its metropolitan agency for the CMA was to be much more powerful.[21] By this time, the Saint-Jérôme area had been added to the northern part of the Montreal CMA, but the Bédard Commission recommended that it not be included. In 2000, the Parti québécois minister of municipal affairs, Louise Harel, introduced legislation establishing a new, but fairly weak, metropolitan authority to be called the Montreal Metropolitan Community (MMC). She accepted the main features of the boundaries proposed by the Bédard Commission. Presumably to avoid being criticized for using boundaries originally drawn by a federal government agency, she claimed that the same procedures for drawing CMA boundaries were used in all industrialized countries. However, she added three municipalities to the northeasterly boundaries of the CMA because they included the port of Contrecoeur, which she considered as an extension of the Port of Montreal.[22] A few months later, another law removed from the MMC one municipality (Lavaltrie) located across the St Lawrence River from Contrecoeur and another one (Saint-Placide) further to the southwest.[23] The next year another municipality (Saint-Jean-Baptiste) was added.[24] None of these territorial changes provoked any debate within Quebec's National Assembly. Whatever motivated them, it is clear that the original plan to replicate the boundaries of the Montreal CMA proved not to be politically possible. In 2006, Statistics Canada added five municipalities to the CMA, only one of which (Verchères) is a member of the MMC. Legislation from Quebec will be needed if they are to join the MMC, but its introduction is far from automatic. In any event, the Montreal Metropolitan Community has done very little since its creation and its boundaries make very little difference to anybody. The fact that it has not been possible for the Quebec government to stick with CMA boundaries even in these unique circumstances illustrates how difficult it would be to adopt CMA boundaries for any stronger form of city-region governance.

Calgary, Alberta, is one of the very few cities in North America that has been able to expand its boundaries through incremental annexations such that almost all (91.6 per cent in 2006) of the population of its CMA (1,079,310 in 2006) has remained within its municipal boundaries.[25] Some of these annexations have been controversial and have generated intense opposition. Decisions on annexation applications from cities in Alberta are made by a quasi-judicial body, the Municipal Government Board (MGB), formerly the Local Authorities Board (LAB). The usual pattern in the past has been for Calgary to ask for very large annexations and for the LAB to grant less than what was requested.[26]

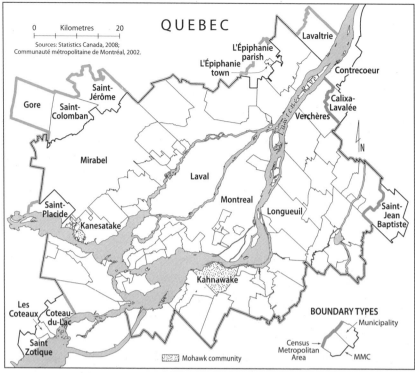

Map 5   The Montreal CMA and the territory of the Montreal Metropolitan Community (MMC)

The official position of the city of Calgary is that it should maintain, at the least, a thirty-year supply of developable land within its boundaries. Having this land supply allows for the long-term planning necessary to accommodate Calgary's rapid rate of growth and facilitates the planning and budgeting of infrastructure (sewers, roads). Periodic annexations are proposed in order to maintain a long-term land supply. The city claims that its annexation policy is a key part of its growth management strategy: "It helps ensure that sprawl does not occur, that is, haphazard development, often at very low density. Calgary's planned suburban communities now achieve densities of 6 to 8 dwelling units per acre. This is almost 40% denser than communities built in the 1970's and 1980's."[27]

Calgary's strategy has been greatly aided in the recent past by the absence of any significant nearby urban municipalities to impede its outward expansion.[28] What the city of Calgary now must recognize, and take account of, is that its current boundaries are coming closer and closer to non-contiguous urban municipalities. Such places as Airdrie, Crossfield, Cochrane, Chestermere, and Okotoks are growing even faster than Calgary itself. The more Calgary grows, the more its neighbouring municipalities will grow and the more they will become integrated into the urban area that is focused on Calgary as the central city. The strategic choice that Calgary faces is whether it should work co-operatively with these urban governments or whether it should absorb them as part of a continuing commitment to including all of the CMA within its boundaries. If it chooses the latter course of action, future annexation battles will be considerably more difficult than those it has won in the past. If it chooses the former, Calgary's inter-municipal issues and problems will start to resemble those of other major metropolitan areas in North America and Europe.

CONCLUSION

The more an urban municipality grows and the more diverse and dynamic its economy becomes, the less likely it is that its boundaries will be able to expand to include all of the built-up area. This state of affairs often leads to proposals for various forms of two-tier metropolitan governments, but these proposals have problems of their own, not the least of which is reaching agreement on the outer boundaries for such a government. Many central-government statistical agencies attempt to define metropolitan areas for statistical purposes.

There is a natural temptation – succumbed to by Gerald Frug in his proposals for regional assemblies in the United States – to use these boundaries for metropolitan governments. This approach was taken in Montreal in 2000, but so far the results have not been encouraging.

Municipal boundaries, even if they result from judicial or quasi-judicial determinations, are the result of compromise. They rarely, if ever, reflect the rational calculations of land-use planners, urban economists, or specialists in urban governance. More than we often care to admit, municipal boundaries appear to have about as much logic as the arbitrary lines drawn through Africa by the various colonial powers. In many urban areas, they continue to exist for much the same reasons as Africa's arbitrary boundaries do. Questioning them can cause more problems than continuing to accept them, and in any event, reaching agreement on alternatives is practically impossible. Ironically, the very existence of a boundary, no matter how arbitrary it might seem, helps shape and determine the nature of the political community that evolves within it. This is just one of the many ways in which the municipal boundaries of cities are similar to those of sovereign states.

4

City-States in Theory and Practice

If more city-states are going to be created in the world, they will have to secede from existing nation-states (sovereign countries), just as Singapore seceded from Malaysia in 1965. And as I have already noted, we might also contemplate new city-states that secede from units of a federation so as to create new federal units. If Toronto seceded from Ontario, for example, the result would be a new Canadian city-state that was also a province. Such secessions raise huge issues, both in theory and in practice. The object of this chapter is to examine these issues.

SECEDING FROM SOVEREIGN STATES

There is now a burgeoning literature in political philosophy relating to the circumstances under which secession is morally justified. Almost all of it is concerned with the rights of national minorities who find themselves trapped within states that are dominated by other national groups.[1] Because no one has claimed that city-regions themselves generate the kind of political loyalty we associate with nations, such literature is mostly irrelevant to the issues of concern here, although it is important to reiterate that one of the most important reasons for Singapore's secession was that its ethnic majority was Chinese, while the rest of Malaysia was dominated by Malays.

Secessionist movements have gained strength in various parts of the world precisely because they have been fuelled by ethnic nationalism. Arguably, movements for autonomy for cities have not gained such strength because attachment to cities is not nearly as politically salient as attachment to an ethnic group. No one has yet been bold enough to suggest exactly how nation-states might make way for city-states, but the idea seems to be that it will either be a gradual process or that it will come about as the result of some kind of agreement among various political leaders, although it is hard to see how such agreement could be implemented without popular approval in a referendum. Whatever the case, imagining the process by which city-states might be created is extremely difficult, even if we assume (contrary to the main argument of this book) that reaching agreement on boundaries would not be a problem.

Let us assume in the first instance that secessionists dominate politically within a large and prosperous city of about 5 million people in a large but not quite so prosperous country of about 50 million. The answer from the central government to any demand for secession would inevitably be negative. The secessionists might hold their own referendum and win overwhelmingly, but is there any reason why should they expect the central government to even negotiate? And should the secessionists expect any degree of international support or recognition? Until recently they could not even draw on political philosophers for support.

But the work of Christopher Heath Wellman opens the door, even though it makes no reference to cities. Wellman's approach is most easily encountered in his 2005 book entitled *A Theory of Secession*. Unlike other theorists of secession, Wellman does not argue that secession can only be justified by claims about the need for national self-determination. He argues that any territorially contiguous group of people within a state should have the right to define a territory in which a referendum would be held to determine if the territory will secede. The decision should be taken by a simple majority of those voting, but Wellman acknowledges that it might be desirable to insist that there be at least two referendums to ensure that any such action is indeed the clear will of the majority.[2] The only condition on the right to secession by referendum is that "both the separatist group and the rump state are capable of maintaining a secure and just political environment." Wellman calls this a "functional" theory of secession because it requires that, after secession, the resulting states be capable of carrying out their most basic of functions – "maintaining a secure and just political environment."[3]

Like many other theorists of secession, Wellman refuses to accept the existing, officially defined territorial units of a state as having a status in relation to secession that is superior to that of other, unofficial territories.[4] For Wellman, municipal and statistical boundaries would be irrelevant in determining any possible secession of a city. It is tempting to classify Wellman's views as anarchistic, but unlike Magnusson,[5] for example, Wellman insists that he is a "statist" because he accepts that "the state appears to be the only effective vehicle to maintain peace and protect rights, because such peace and security requires a territorial monopoly of power that cannot be achieved if everyone's consent is required."[6] This is why, even with what seems like an almost unlimited right to secession, some people are going to be trapped in a state of which they do not approve. A single family living in a suburban house – even one with a large lot – cannot meet Wellman's criteria for statehood. It is quite possible, however, that a few dozen of such families, especially if they were rich, might be able to. Whether they would be wise to attempt statehood is, of course, another matter. In any event, Wellman avoids having to make such tough determinations by assuming that secessions would have to be approved by an international court, a heroic assumption that comes close to assuming that there is already a world government and that the court, when evaluating secession proposals, would simply be refereeing between administrative subdivisions.

Wellman also claims that the court would not be overburdened because, once the right to secede was accepted, the need actually to assert that right would be dramatically reduced. He supports this claim by referring to Canada: "[T]here is every reason to expect that the number of those who favour an independent Quebec will actually decrease in the coming years as Canada continues to respect Quebec's right to political self-determination and its own national sovereignty becomes less important."[7]

Theoretically interesting as Wellman's argument might be, it is not especially useful to advocates of city-states. As already noted, he makes no reference to cities and clearly does not privilege their territories in any way. If Wellman's scheme were implemented, it is possible that cities would gain political power, either by seceding or by threatening to secede. More likely, however, is the possibility that cities themselves would be undermined by secessionist movements within existing municipal boundaries or statistical metropolitan areas. Although academics and consultants have frequently extolled the growing role of cities on the world's stage, in practical political terms, local agitation for new suburban municipal incorporations and for secessions from existing municipalities has outstripped any popular political support for increased political authority for urban municipalities or metropolitan government.

Under Wellman's scheme, it would be easier for residents of the San Fernando Valley to secede from the United States than it would be for them, under current California law, to secede from the City of Los Angeles. California law allows secession referendums, but the plan must be approved by a majority of voters in the entire city. Voters in the San Fernando Valley have themselves approved secession from Los Angeles, but voters in the city as a whole have rejected it.[8] Robert Young warns us against conflating municipal secessions and secessions from sovereign states: the latter are likely to lead to great political and economic uncertainty and potential armed conflict, while the former "centre around relatively mild resentment about tax levels and services."[9]

Ironically, Wellman's entire argument seems to relate more to "mild resentment" than to the passions that are aroused by proposals to break up existing nation-states. Like Magnusson and many other analysts from different political perspectives who advocate or predict the demise of the sovereign nation-state, Wellman simply does not account for the importance of the nation-state as the organizing basis for our political lives. By any objective standard, the Canadian federal government must be one of the weakest national governments in the developed world. After transfers to the provinces, it spends less than half of the total annual government spending in the country. The national government delivers few services directly to citizens and has only a limited role in policy-making for health, education, and social services. There is a very strong secessionist movement in Quebec and much alienation in the West. But even many apparent supporters of Quebec sovereignty do not want to "destroy Canada" or lose their Canadian passports. They certainly do not want a new Quebec currency. Outside Quebec, most Canadians desperately want to keep the entire country together, from sea to sea to sea. The maple leaf flag and public health insurance, both only forty years old as of this writing, are powerful symbols of a distinct national identity. To varying degrees, residents of Toronto, Vancouver, and Calgary might recognize and accept that global institutions, free-trade agreements, and their own provincial and city governments have become more important in their lives than the Canadian national government based in Ottawa. But the notions that Canadian sovereignty might somehow disappear or that Quebec might secede – let alone the idea that their province or their city-region might secede – are imagined as forms of political catastrophe. If this is the case in Canada, it must be more so in just about every other region of the developed world. Even so, there are indeed countries other than Canada that must contend with nationalist secessionist movements. But secessions of cities from sovereign states are not on the political horizon anywhere.

SECEDING FROM STATES AND PROVINCES

As we saw earlier, the last time there was secession from an American state was in 1863, when West Virginia was carved out of Virginia during the American Civil War. There have been no secessions from provinces in Canada.

Section 3 of article 4 of the US constitution states that "no new State shall be formed or erected within the Jurisdiction of any other State; nor any State be formed by the Junction of two or more States, or Parts of States, without the Consent of the Legislatures of the States concerned as well as of the Congress." Even in the unlikely event that a state legislature would approve the breakup of its own state, it is even less likely that Congress would approve. The net effect of such approval would be to allocate two additional senators to the area of the state that was being divided. If New York City could attain two senators for itself, that would be reason enough to secede from New York State. But that is precisely why congressional approval would not be forthcoming. Even Gerald Frug, who contemplates dramatic shifts of authority within American states and local governments, does not propose any secessions or alterations in state boundaries so as to accommodate his concerns about city-regions.[10] He knows that such proposals would be far less attainable than the radical proposals he already is advancing. There will be no city-states within the United States in the foreseeable future.

The creation of a new Canadian province from territory within an existing province would require the approval of the legislature of the province, the legislatures of seven other provinces representing 50 per cent of the Canadian population, and the Parliament of Canada. This is not going to happen. But let us assume that, for one reason or another, agreement would be forthcoming in the rest of Canada for whatever might be decided within Ontario on the issue of breaking up the country's largest province. Apart from Toronto, the most credible case for secession is found in northern Ontario. The new northern province would take with it less than 10 per cent of the population. The area's population is currently declining, and its fiscal position would be weak. The new entity would contain two major cities (Greater Sudbury and Thunder Bay) of over 100,000 people separated by Georgian Bay and Lake Superior. However, such a secession would have nothing to do with cities. There is just as much reason to split northern Ontario into two provinces as there is to split Ontario itself (or, as we have seen in chapter 2, to attach northwestern Ontario to Manitoba). In any event, let us also assume that southern Ontario is left on its own and that there is a movement in and around Toronto for a Toronto-based secession.

One possibility is that the territory of the existing city of Toronto could secede.[11] Indeed, there is a small group of supporters for precisely this option. Their candidates for mayor won 0.04 and 0.08 per cent, respectively, of the popular vote in the mayoral elections of 2003 and 2006.[12] Precisely because the city of Toronto does have defined boundaries, a mayor and council, and its own fiscal resources, it is at least possible to imagine a disgruntled, charismatic mayor convincing his or her constituents that secession would be a good idea. In financial terms, city taxpayers would probably be better off than they are now. The city's population would make it the fifth-largest province in Canada, behind the rest of Ontario, Quebec, British Columbia, and Alberta.

The main problem with such a plan is that it would bifurcate the Toronto city-region. The city of Toronto's boundaries run through densely populated areas, and turning them into provincial boundaries would surely create more problems than it would solve. The writings of Jane Jacobs, Kenichi Ohmae, Neal Peirce, and many others are about the economic importance of cities and their regions,[13] not about the importance of central-city municipalities, no matter how

populous they might be as a result of past municipal amal-
gamations. Many argue that the 1998 amalgamation that
created the current city of Toronto did nothing to improve
the governance arrangements for the wider city-region of
Toronto. Using these same boundaries to create a new province would exacerbate the original problem. The largest
municipality remaining in Ontario would be the city of Mississauga, immediately to the west of the new province of
Toronto. Suburban Toronto would become the population
centre of Ontario, a state of affairs that makes no sense from
any perspective.

As we saw in chapter 1, Alan Broadbent proposes that a
territory roughly similar to what Statistics Canada calls the
"Extended Golden Horseshoe" should secede from Ontario.
This proposal makes much more sense than the proposal that
only the city of Toronto secede. However, it seems highly unlikely that residents in the outer periphery would vote to join
a new province in which Toronto city dwellers would be so
dominant. If these residents did indeed vote against seceding
along with Toronto to form a new province, there is no conceivable reason why they should be forced to do so. If the
outer periphery did not join Toronto, why should residents of
the inner suburbs, such as Mississauga, agree?

One answer might be that a prosperous province of
Toronto would keep a much higher proportion of its tax
revenues within its borders, making it possible that Toronto
taxes could be significantly lowered. Such a prospect would
presumably have considerable appeal to suburban voters,
but its corollary would be that residents of the rest of Ontario would face higher taxes in order to maintain the same
level of government services. Why should they ever agree
to Toronto secession?

This question raises the "remnant" problem, a problem at the heart of any proposal for city-states. Toronto is the focal point for the entire region. Southern Ontario without Toronto is a remnant; it is not in any sense a meaningful political unit. The only way that the remnant problem could be solved would be to establish simultaneously mini-city-states for southwestern Ontario, presumably centred on London, and at least one other one in eastern Ontario, presumably centred on Ottawa. Of course, if Ottawa were to be a real city-state, it would have to include a huge amount of the territory of western Quebec, thus sparking a new round of impossible boundary negotiations. Even with all this boundary re-engineering, the remnant problem would still not be solved: significant areas that would not be included within the Extended Golden Horseshoe would have a much greater connection with Toronto than with either Ottawa or London. Such areas largely coincide with Toronto's "cottage country," that is, northern Simcoe County, Parry Sound–Muskoka, Haliburton County, and Kawartha Lakes. Even the city of Peterborough and Peterborough County are much more naturally linked with Toronto than with Ottawa.

A secession movement based in Toronto is doomed to failure because there can never be agreement on what constitutes Toronto. An alternative possibility could be that the government of Ontario would recognize the desirability of dividing the province and would establish some form of royal commission to decide on the number of units and their boundaries. Such a commission could well recommend a new province for northern Ontario (which clearly would not be a city-state) and three new provinces (or city-states) centred on Toronto, Ottawa, and London. Arguably, there would be no need for popular approval by referendum for the creation of the four new provinces. Ontario would simply make the proposal to the federal government and the other provinces and hope that they would agree that, in future federal-provincial conferences, the current territory of Ontario would be represented by four premiers rather than one.

Let us make one more heroic assumption: this proposal for sectioning up Ontario is approved. The province of Ontario is replaced by four new provinces, and this is done primarily, we must recall, to ensure that Canada's largest city, Toronto, attains a measure of self-government not previously available to it. Given that our hypothetical province of Toronto includes a territory more extensive than any previous geographical delimitation, it might well be that some central Torontonians, initially enthusiastic about a city-state, would feel that their original objective is being undermined by the inclusion of so many far-flung and non-urban residents. Even if this were so, they could console themselves with the knowledge that their new province is at least much more compact and Toronto-centred than the old province of Ontario was.

But there is one more issue to consider. Notwithstanding the fact that these boundary changes would be the most significant in the history of Canada and Ontario, the process would not be over. As long as it remains prosperous, the Toronto city-region will not stop growing. Even if urban sprawl is slowed by greenbelts and intensification, a growing Toronto will increasingly attract commuters from established communities that are even further afield. Statistics Canada already considers Kitchener-Waterloo, Barrie, and St Catharines to be part of the Extended Golden Horseshoe. Surely it is not unrealistic to expect that commuting patterns will change within the next few decades to include London as well. Would the London area then be included within the province of Toronto? What would happen to the new London-centred province? If the boundaries were not changed, they could one day be seen as being just as arbitrary and inimical to the interests of city-regions as some American state boundaries are (an analogy would be the Boston city-region, which clearly extends into southern New Hampshire). There is one simple truth here: permanent boundaries cannot be drawn around dynamic city-regions.

All of the potential problems and pitfalls involving a Toronto city-state can be easily avoided by *not* attempting to divide Ontario, certainly not southern Ontario anyway. In the next chapter, we will look at how city-regions can be governed within our existing structures of government, but first we should address one more issue as we contemplate the secession of city-states.

CITY-STATES AND LOCAL GOVERNMENT

Some people might be tempted to support the secession of city-states if for no other reason than they want their government to be simpler and more accountable. The assumption is that a city-state would comprise one government that would look after everything. No longer would there be two or more layers of government, including local governments, with much confusion about exactly who is in charge of what. Such an assumption is mistaken.

If it were only the central-city municipality that seceded, then arguably there could be only one government. But such a government would have to enter into hundreds of "interprovincial" agreements just to maintain the basic urban infrastructure, such as roads, public-transit facilities and routes, water-supply systems, and a host of other such items. In addition, there would be a range of new issues. Could Toronto plumbers do their work outside the city-state. What about teacher accreditation? Who would handle paperwork for health insurance? All these issues could readily be solved, but not without creating new agreements, protocols, procedures, and approval processes. In short, the one new government would generate much new red tape.

If the boundaries were more extensive, as I believe would be necessary to capture the advantages of having a city-state, then the need for local government quickly becomes apparent. No one would want the central legislature to have to wrestle with a controversial zoning issue in a downtown neighbourhood, especially not the residents of the neighbourhood, who would likely have little faith that representatives from the outer periphery would have any understanding of their local concerns. Similarly, downtown representatives would have little interest in solving drainage problems in rural areas. More importantly, the demand for local public services would inevitably be higher in the more densely populated urban areas because dense urban living generates externalities that require collective action.[14] Such problems can be mitigated by the creation of local governments, which would offer informed governmental responses in different local situations. City-states would need local governments just as much as any other state does. As always, however, relations between the central and local governments would be complex and often difficult.

CITY-STATES
IN THE EUROPEAN FEDERATIONS

City-states have not seceded in Germany, Austria, and Switzerland. They have existed for a very long time, notwithstanding considerable pressure, especially in Germany, for them to merge with the units that have surrounded them. They remain because their leaders and residents have resisted change. Madrid and Brussels, as I have noted, have more recently been established as units within the new federal states of Spain and Belgium, but their creation had little to with deliberate plans to establish new city-states. Regardless of the reasons for the existence of Europe's city-states, it is important to understand their impact on city governance, if for no other reason than that such city-state arrangements seem so attractive to observers elsewhere – in Toronto, for example.

We have already seen that, in Germany, *Land* boundaries have been a matter of considerable controversy, much of it relating to the three city-states of Hamburg, Bremen, and Berlin. No one argues that the consolidation of municipal and *Land* functions within the city-state is itself a cause of any problems. The potential problems relate to the external boundaries. Indeed, it has twice been seriously proposed that Hamburg and Bremen should be absorbed into Lower Saxony. The first such proposal, in the 1950s, was rejected, in part because it would have meant further political isolation for West Berlin, leaving it as the only city-state in West Germany. A similar proposal was made in the 1970s, but this time party politics were more obviously a factor. Hamburg and Bremen have both been strongholds of the Social Democrats. Their absorption into Lower Saxony would upset long-standing patterns of party control in all three territories. Furthermore, Helmut Schmidt, a federal Social Democratic cabinet minister (later the chancellor) from Hamberg, was not going to allow the *Land* of Hamburg to disappear.[15] Bremen's status was in turn protected by Hamburg's. As noted previously, *Land* boundaries in the territory of the former West Germany have not changed since 1952.

Map 6 Berlin, Bremen, and Hamburg: cities as *Länder* in Germany

In Bremen, there is a separate municipal government for Bremerhaven, which is part of the *Land* of Bremen even though sixty-five kilometres of territory within Lower Saxony separates it from the city of Bremen.[16] This territorial anomaly dates back to 1826 and is one of the more obvious reasons why a restructuring of *Land* boundaries has frequently been a significant item of political debate and conflict. But for our purposes the most important issues relate to the extent to which the external boundaries of the city-states correspond to the territory of their respective built-up urban areas. In all three of these German city-states, urban growth has extended beyond the official boundaries, thereby creating intergovernmental issues familiar to any student of urban politics.

Anyone who believes that the creation of city-states in itself simplifies urban government should consider this statement:

The city of Hamburg is the core of a metropolitan region in NW Germany encompassing some 4 million people and straddling 3 state boundaries and 14 counties, each with a

number of local authorities. Because of this multitude
of administrative territories, including a city-state and
two federal states ... the Hamburg area has over the years
become something of a test case of inter-local, cross-
border co-operation, both formal and informal.[17]

There is now a good case to be made that metropolitan Hamburg also extends into the western part of the former East
German *Land* of Mecklenburg-Vorpommern (Mecklenberg–
Western Pomerania, in English), which is less than eighty kilometres from the city.[18]

Had the Third Reich not expanded Hamburg through the
amalgamation of adjoining municipalities,[19] the population
of the Hamburg *Land* would be considerably less than its 1.7
million of 2008. But even with these extended boundaries,
metropolitan planning institutions involving each of the
neighbouring *Länder* of Schleswig-Holstein and Lower Saxony were established as early as the 1950s. These arrangements, after considerable conflict and at times neglect,
evolved during the early 1990s to become a single organization known as "Metropolregion Hamburg," which then
produced a "Regional Development Concept."[20] Although
this organization has had its successes – for example, outlying counties have been anxious to attach themselves to it because of its apparent success in promoting economic
development – Hamburg takes the position that regional-
ization has been more of a benefit to the outlying areas than
to itself. For this reason it has occasionally been reluctant to
commit funds to the organization.[21]

The *Land* of Bremen (excluding Bremerhaven) has a population of .55 million; its metropolitan region is 2.3 million.[22]
Like Hamburg, the territory of the *Land* was expanded during

the Third Reich, but postwar growth extended it further out-
wards into Lower Saxony. A joint planning board was established by the two *Länder* in 1965. This bi-state planning board
evolved into the Regionale Arbeitgemeinschaft Bremen/
Niedersachsen, which involves municipalities in Lower Saxony as well as the *Land* government.[23]

Joachim Blatter sums up the Hamburg and Bremen experience in these words: "[W]e are witnessing a multiplication
of identities of the central city-states and concentric circles
of cooperation and joint decision-making (always covering
many functional fields). Hamburg and Bremen no longer
define themselves only as *Länder* ... They now accept their
identities as municipalities and cooperate directly with their
suburban counterparts."[24] Blatter's analysis includes four
other German metropolitan regions (Frankfurt, Munich,
Stuttgart, and Hanover). Significantly, he sees these city-
states as a relatively unimportant variable. Their existence
has been an obstacle to cooperation in the past, but one that
has obviously not been insurmountable.

The political situation in the city-state of Berlin has been
much more complicated. During the Cold War, West Berlin
was a separate *Land* within West Germany. After German
reunification in 1989, it was obvious that the city of Berlin
would be administratively reunited, but the big issue was
whether it would continue as a separate *Land* or be merged
with the surrounding *Land* of Brandenburg. For most German observers, the experiences of the "administratively divided city regions" of Hamburg and Bremen as city-states
should best be avoided: "Their [Hamburg's and Bremen's]
forty years' experience in arranging – with varying success
– cooperation between the two *Land* governments demon-
strated the difficulties of such arrangements, and it seemed

opportune to ... consider a rapid move towards merging the two separate entities [Berlin and Brandenburg]."[25] A referendum was held in Berlin and Brandenburg in 1996 on the issue of merging the two *Länder*. The merger was supported by political elites in both jurisdictions who were concerned about providing appropriate infrastructure to manage Berlin's outward expansion. The referendum was also seen by some as a potential harbinger of territorial restructuring for other *Länder*. Voters in the former West Berlin ended up supporting the merger, but their counterparts in the former East Berlin and in Brandenburg voted against it and carried the day. The former East Germans were highly suspicious that the merger would lead to domination by the West Berliners. The defeat of the merger has meant that the governance of the Berlin city-region now involves many of the sort of arrangements that have been worked out for Hamburg and Bremen.[26] The main contextual difference is that Berlin is relatively much more dominant in its city-region than Hamburg and Bremen are in theirs. Its population is 3.6 million, while the population of all of Brandenburg is only 2.6 million. The largest municipality in Brandenburg is its capital, Potsdam, whose population is only 130,000.[27]

It is important to note that Berlin, unlike Hamburg and Bremen, is divided into twelve districts, each of which elects its own council.

The districts are responsible for such matters as schools, adult education, hospitals, libraries, swimming facilities, youth homes, athletic fields, parks, and music schools. Delegated matters under supervision include building plans, street maintenance and lighting, elections, and

property issues. The districts can make their own zoning
plans and they enjoy some fiscal autonomy.[28]

There is apparently very little co-operation between Berlin's
outlying districts and the neighbouring municipalities in
Brandenburg.[29]

All three German city-states have territories that are too
small to cover their continuous built-up areas, let alone the
economic hinterland of their city-regions. Although politicians within Hamburg and Bremen have fought hard to retain their historical status, it appears that there are few, if
any, observers within Germany who would support the
German city-state model as an effective mechanism for the
governance of city-regions. The situation is remarkably similar in Vienna. Although its *Land* dates back only to the
1920s, following the dissolution of the Austro-Hungarian
Empire,[30] its constitutional status within Austria is similar
to that of Hamburg, Bremen, and Berlin within Germany.
Vienna is both a *Land* and a municipality. Like the German
city-states, however, its territory does not include the entire
metropolitan area. The population of the *Land* is about 1.6
million, but that of the metropolitan area is 2.2 million. Unlike the German city-states, the Vienna *Land* has virtually no
links with its neighbouring metropolitan municipalities in
the *Land* of Lower Austria. Indeed, prosperous municipalities to the south of Vienna are competing effectively in attracting new businesses to the area. One such municipality
has "become increasingly attractive as a result of the eastward expansion of the European Union."[31]

On the surface, it would appear that Switzerland is another
promising location for city-states. The Swiss Federal Office of
Statistics identifies five metropolitan areas in Switzerland:

Zurich, Geneva, Basel, Berne, and Ticino. Each is located within a canton (province) of the same name. However, according to the Office of Statistics, the territory of only one of them, Berne, is located solely within its own canton. The population of each of the other metropolitan areas is spread over at least two cantons, and in the case of Basel, it is spread over three different countries (Switzerland, Germany, and France). The largest of the Swiss metropolitan areas, Zurich, has a population of about 1.5 million located in six different cantons and 172 different communes (municipalities). The metropolitan area of Berne has a total population of only about 0.4 million. Switzerland may well be an exemplar of grassroots democracy, but no one can claim that it harbours large and powerful city-states.[32]

Belgium adopted a federal constitution in 1989.[33] One of the three constituent territorial units is Brussels, leading to the natural thought that it might be another candidate for city-state status.[34] But everyone agrees that the creation of the Brussels capital region had nothing to do with self-government for city-regions and everything to do with arriving at a territorial compromise that the country's two major ethnic groups, the Flemish and the Walloons, could live with. Even the statistical definition of the Brussels metropolitan area is a contentious political issue: "French [Walloon] research centres are mostly in favour of a maximum and Dutch [Flemish] centres of a minimum delimitation. The underlying fear of the latter is the political linking of the notion [of] 'socio-economic metropolitan region' to the extension of the bilingual region."[35] Despite these conflicts and uncertainties, I present the following numbers to convey some idea of the scales we are discussing: the formal capital region has a population of 0.96 million and covers

162 km²; the "morphological agglomeration" has 1.3 million inhabitants and covers 529 km²; and the "agglomeration and periphery" has 1.9 million people and covers 1401 km².[36] Because of the political tensions, "a global planning approach to the metropolitan region of Brussels seems to be an institutional impossibility," so "most problems are solved during informal, pragmatic consultations."[37] But such consultations can be very difficult because of the problematic location of the boundaries. For example, the ring road around Brussels is 72 km long, and all but only 12 km are within the territory of Flanders. Similarly, the Brussels airport is located within Flanders.[38] No one interested in self-government for city-regions would possibly design a city-state with these boundaries.

Like Belgium, Spain is another European country that has recently become federalized. Although Spain clearly has its own ethnic tensions, they are not reflected within any particular city or metropolitan region, as in Brussels. More by accident than design, this has meant that Spain has emerged with governments of "autonomous communities" that arguably are close to the ideal arrangements for self-governing city-regions. Barcelona has been the Spanish city that has received the most attention from the international media. For a while, it also received attention from students of urban government because a metropolitan level of government was established for Barcelona that looked as though it could serve as a possible model for elsewhere in Europe. But this level was abolished in 1988 as a result of a conflict with the increasingly powerful government of the autonomous community of Catalonia. The population of Catalonia is about 6.2 million, while that of metropolitan Barcelona is 4.4 million.[39] There is a real sense in which metropolitan Barcelona *is* Catalonia, but because of the historic and apparently successful battles to preserve Catalan national identity, no one wants to conceptualize the Catalan autonomous community as a form of city-state: Catalonia is a nation, not a city.

Unlike Barcelona, Madrid has its own autonomous community. But this was not the result of anyone's deliberate plan to establish Madrid as a city-state. It was more the result of people living in Castilla La Mancha (the region in which Madrid has been traditionally located) wanting in the 1970s to separate themselves from the problems of the capital city. As Jane Jacobs notes in *Cities and the Wealth of Nations*, Madrid is not the centre of a dynamic city-region. Instead it is an isolated city 650 metres above sea level in the middle of the Iberian Plateau. Once outside the continuous built-up area, "one has to travel more than 200 km to find a city with more than 100,000 inhabitants, and 350 km to reach the nearest seaport."[40] This means that, however one defines Madrid's territory, it is included within the autonomous region.

In 1996, the autonomous community of Madrid had a population of just over 5 million. All but about 100,000 people lived in the metropolitan area or its rapidly suburbanizing immediate periphery. This situation caused Jesús Leal Maldonado to write the following, the kind of commentary that is almost unheard of in any study of urban governance in democratic countries:

[T]he Functional Urban Region of Madrid fits the space of the Autonomous Community ... This fact is important because the city-community of Madrid is a strong institution with many resources and competencies to govern its urban region. It facilitates the coordination between the municipalities and contributes to the definition of a singular urban policy for all the municipalities that come under this unitary political power.[41]

Madrid is the exceptional case: a city-region with its own powerful government in charge of urban planning, transportation, housing, health, and education – all the functional and financial responsibilities required to govern a large city. Madrid, of course, is not without its problems. The central area has been losing population, and the outer suburban ring of municipalities has been growing very rapidly.[42] The 179 municipalities within the autonomous community "have limited resources and limited capacity (one of the lowest in Europe) and the opportunities for citizen involvement are still limited."[43]

If the citizens of the Madrid autonomous community want to make their municipalities stronger, they can do so through their elected community government. All the right structures are in place. To what extent can the Madrid experience be emulated in other federations? Unfortunately, the prospects are not good. First, we would have to find a city that is isolated from others and that has not generated an economically dynamic region of its own such that there are many smaller towns and cities in the immediate hinterland. Second, in the case of Madrid, the prospects for establishing expansive boundaries for a new city-state were greatly facilitated by the fact that there was a unique opportunity to restructure the Spanish state in the 1980s as it emerged from decades of dictatorship. Established federations rarely offer such opportunities. Changing the boundaries of their constituent units, as we have seen, is next to impossible.

CONCLUSION

Advocates of the secession of cities from existing jurisdictions receive little support from political philosophers. Cities, the political theorists say, have no claim to national self-determination. Theories of secession that do not rely on concepts related to nationhood, culture, and language provide a potential justification of city secession, but they also provide justification for the secession of disaffected areas within cities, thereby causing as many potential problems as solutions. In practice, secession is fraught with constitutional problems as well as with the kind of boundary problems that are at the heart of this book. Finally, the real city-states within the European federations, with one exception, must cope with boundaries that do not include all of their respective metropolitan areas, which usually leads to the kind of complex intergovernmental institutions and arrangements found in growing city-regions throughout the world. Madrid is the exception that proves the rule.

Cities and Central Governments

If there are not to be city-states, then how are cities to be governed? Such a question takes us back to more familiar terrain, but the answers are not any easier. Indeed, one of the main attractions of the city-state idea is that it appears to simplify urban government. In theory, the creation of city-states would dramatically reduce the need for complex intergovernmental negotiations and arrangements. In practice, as we have seen, most city-states create intergovernmental problems of their own. As we discuss relations between urban municipalities and their central governments, we shall have to accept complexity as a natural part of urban governance.

CITIES IN LARGE UNITARY STATES

France and Britain (England, at least) are large unitary states. The absence of federalism is probably both a cause and a result of the fact that each of these countries is dominated by one large urban centre, Paris and London respectively. Because these two cities are so dominant, central-government policies that affect development in each of them also affect the entire territory of their respective countries. Indeed, one of the most important perennial policy challenges facing the central governments of France and England is having to find a way to balance the interests of the dominant city against those of the "provincial" or "regional" cities. Such a challenge comes to the fore in just about any government decision relating to infrastructure, transportation, and economic development. The emergence of Paris and London as global cities makes such policy problems even more politically difficult. Should the emphasis be on enhancing the global competitiveness of these cities or on having them share their wealth with other less fortunate cities within their country?

Large unitary states are by definition saddled with such challenges. To meet them, states must design systems of local government and regional representation that enable different cities within the country both to make decisions for themselves and to be heard in central institutions. Much academic attention has been focused on how such systems have evolved in France and Britain.[1] To put it simply, French cities have relied on the emergence of powerful local leaders within the various political parties who simultaneously hold office locally, regionally, and nationally, while the British have paid much more attention to rearranging local-government institutions and boundaries such that urban conurbations at least have the theoretical capacity to make decisions for themselves. We need not be concerned with which system seems to work best. The key point is that a crucial task of the central governments is to balance the interests of different cities in the context of there being one dominant city.

Federalism lessens the burden of urban policy-making on central governments because most (but not all) urban issues are under the jurisdiction of the regional units of government.

My argument throughout this book has been that, even in the absence of the kind of near-perfect regional-unit boundaries such as are found in Madrid, we should accept regional units as the central policy-making institutions for cities within federations. The rest of the analysis in this chapter applies to the constituent units within federations or to relatively small unitary states such as the Netherlands, Portugal, Greece, and the Scandinavian countries.

CITY-REGIONS AND THEIR CENTRAL GOVERNMENTS

I have argued earlier that defining the boundaries of city-regions is exceptionally difficult, even for agencies charged only with collecting statistics relating to city-regions. The problems that Statistics Canada has in defining Toronto's city-region illustrate this point perfectly. The first imperative for central governments as they confront urban policy-making is to recognize that there is no single acceptable definition of any large city-region. In some jurisdictions, one city-region is obviously dominant; in some respects, its urban influence covers the entire territory of the jurisdiction and probably beyond. Sydney's city-region in New South Wales, Australia, Chicago's in Illinois, and Vancouver's in British Columbia are striking examples. In other cases, there are at least two competing city-regions in the same jurisdiction and none of them totally dominates. Los Angeles and San Francisco in California, Edmonton and Calgary in Alberta, and even Saint John, Moncton, and Fredericton in New Brunswick are examples here.

Neither the state government of California nor the provincial government of Alberta has in recent years been particularly concerned with making explicit policy decisions about urban development. Both have seemed more interested in letting the market prevail. But even an approach such as this amounts to a policy, a policy that in each case probably means that the two dominant city-regions within each of these jurisdictions will continue to sprawl outward towards each other. We have already seen that Statistics Canada has recognized the existence of the "Calgary-Edmonton Corridor." A jurisdiction such as New Brunswick, however, simply does not fit well with the argument I am advancing because the province contains two census metropolitan areas (CMAS) of roughly equal population (Moncton and Saint John) and their combined populations comprise just over a third of the provincial total.[2] This reminds us of what most states and provinces were like before the massive explosion of post-1945 urbanization in most parts of Canada and the United States.

All central governments with significant cities within their territories have to deal with municipal governments that are already established. Their room for manoeuvre in relation to these municipalities varies considerably. For example, Canadian provincial governments (except that of British Columbia) have frequently rearranged municipal boundaries so as to transform, with dramatic results, the pattern of municipal organization within city-regions. Such boundary changes have been much rarer in the United States and have almost never resulted solely from the action of a state legislature.[3]

A frequent justification for such boundary changes and other forms of municipal reorganization relates to the governmental functions that municipalities in the city-region are expected to perform. The argument is that municipalities have to be of a certain minimum size to deliver certain public services effectively or that there has to be a metropolitan-level of government to plan for and build major items of regional infrastructure. I and many others have addressed such issues elsewhere, and the impassioned arguments on each side need not concern us here. My objective now is to examine governmental functions for the city-region in a much broader context. We saw earlier, for example, that Jane Jacobs believed that the government of each city-region should be responsible for its own currency. Drawing appropriate boundaries for a city-region with its own currency is a quite different enterprise from drawing boundaries that might be appropriate for watershed regulation, which in turn is likely to be quite different from drawing boundaries appropriate for the local control of elementary schools. It happens to be the case in Ontario that none of the governmental functions to which I just referred (currencies, watershed regulation, and elementary schools) are under the control of municipal governments. The currency in Ontario is controlled by the federal government, watershed regulation is a responsibility of local special-purpose bodies known as conservation authorities, and elementary schools are the responsibility of four different varieties of school boards (which themselves are also local special-purpose bodies), English public, English Catholic, French public, and French Catholic. Each of these functions is therefore irrelevant to the pattern of municipal organization.

As policy-making for the allocation of resources among public hospitals has become increasingly complex in recent years, many central jurisdictions have attempted to decentralize decision-making so as to ease the pressure at the centre and to be more responsive to local needs. Most jurisdictions have established a network of local special-purpose bodies with relatively large territories to carry out this task. However, in 1999, a provincial commission in Quebec recommended that the allocation of health-care resources be the responsibility of an upper-tier municipal authority covering the entire census metropolitan area of Montreal.[4] Almost every interest and professional group concerned with health opposed this idea, and it was never implemented. Had it been, there would have been a functionally powerful form of municipal government for the Montreal city-region quite unlike any other municipal institution in North America.

In most European countries, municipalities have functional responsibility for what the British call "personal social services." Such services include child protection, services for the developmentally and physically disabled, and various forms of counselling. In Canada, virtually none of these services are the responsibility of municipal governments. They are therefore not relevant to any discussion of municipal organization within city-regions. In Ontario, municipalities still have administrative (and some financial) responsibility for financial assistance to able-bodied residents who have no financial resources, but all the policy decisions concerning such payments are made by the province.

In Canada and the United States, municipalities generally have very little direct responsibility for health and social services or for public education, although in some American municipalities school boards come under varying forms of municipal supervision. Policing is usually a municipal function, but in many jurisdictions various institutional mechanisms insulate the police from direct day-to-day control by mayors and municipal councils. In general, however, municipalities are responsible for governmental functions related to the built environment: infrastructure for transportation and public utilities; parks and public spaces; recreational and cultural facilities; zoning and building regulation; and fire protection.

The assumption is often made that the only governments that are relevant to the governance of city-regions are municipalities. This is wrong on two counts. First, it ignores the role of the central government (or governments in a federal system), a role that is always crucial regardless of how functionally powerful municipalities might be. Less obviously (in Canada at least), such an assumption ignores the existence of local special-purpose bodies, especially for health and education. Regional health authorities seem to be growing in importance and school boards seem to be losing power, although the latter can still make crucial urban decisions about such matters as school closings in areas of declining population. When we take special-purpose bodies into consideration, we do not see only municipal boundaries when we look at territorial issues in city-region governance. Instead we often see a complex network of different boundaries for different authorities and functions.

Let us assume for a moment, however, that we are only concerned about the governance of the built environment within cities. Even if we limit our functional concerns in this way, the issues relating to appropriate governmental structures are remarkably complex. For example, a very large territory is likely to be needed to provide a sewage treatment facility, while neighbourhood parks are likely best managed by an institution responsible for a much smaller territory. As we have seen previously in this book, one possible way of handling this problem is for each city-region to have multiple special-purpose bodies, including one each for sewage treatment and for neighbourhood parks. As far as sewage treatment is concerned, this is precisely what happens in many American cities. In Canada, sewage treatment is generally the direct responsibility of large urban municipalities or of upper-tier metropolitan or regional authorities. Special-purpose bodies for neighbourhood parks are generally non-existent in both countries,[5] but most such parks in the United States are under the jurisdiction of what most Canadian provincial officials would consider to be very small urban municipalities.

In Canada, however, boundaries of large municipalities rarely correspond exactly with the areas covered by a single integrated sewage-treatment system. Some residences in more isolated areas are not covered, while in other places the system transcends municipal boundaries to take in urban areas that have managed to work out some kind of arrangement with their municipal neighbour. For reasons that will be examined briefly later, such arrangements in Canada are often seen as an indicator of things having gone wrong, rather than right.

Operating a sewage-treatment system is a different task than planning for future systems that will be required because of additional urban growth. By definition, the territories required for these two distinct functions do not coincide. It is the perceived need for a city-region authority responsible for planning future infrastructure that is the most compelling reason why some form of multi-functional municipal authority is needed to cover the entire area. The idea is that planning for major roads and major underground pipes needs to be coordinated and that such planning can and should determine the location of future development. Once again, however, the problem is that the ideal territory for planning future sewage-treatment and

water-supply systems is likely not the same as the ideal territory for planning new roads and commuter rail lines. And
it is in the very outermost areas of the city-region, where
there is least likelihood of exact overlap, that the most crucial strategic decisions about new public investments need
to be made.

This is why I contend that the most effective solution to
such problems of city-region governance is for the central
government to look after planning for long-range infrastructural development. Its various ministries might well
set up local advisory bodies, but decisions would rest with
the central government. The more capable the central government is in co-ordinating the programs of its different
ministries within the same city-region, the more effective
such decisions are likely to be.

MUNICIPALITIES AND CITY-REGIONS

Do municipalities themselves have to control piped infrastructure in order to control the pattern of urban development? Or
can such infrastructure be managed by special-purpose authorities – or even publicly regulated private companies – as is
common in the United States? The contention that municipalities must directly control piped infrastructure has often been
an article of faith among land-use planners and municipal officials in Ontario. It is an issue that deserves serious consideration because it has been such an important factor in Canadian
debates about city-region governance. Once this issue is resolved, we can confront other crucial issues relating to the role
of municipalities in the governance of city-regions.

One of the most important theories behind the implementation of metropolitan and regional government in Ontario

from the 1950s to the 1970s was that the best way to plan for and control urban development was to exercise direct control over piped infrastructure. All new and restructured upper-tier local authorities established in this period were granted such authority, the idea being that the availability of piped infrastructure would determine the location of new development. Such an approach was in fact a huge vote of non-confidence in the province's regulatory system for land-use planning. It sent the message that provincial supervision of municipal regulations by itself would not work – specifically, that development could only be controlled if developers were told that they had to go where the pipes were.

The alternative approach – and by far the most common one in North America – is to treat piped infrastructure like any other utility, an example being natural gas: the supplier simply follows the legally approved developments. The supplier could be a local special-purpose body, the central-city municipality, or even a private company. The supplier, of course, would have to have some idea in advance of where future development is likely to take place, but this is exactly the purpose of a forward-looking land-use planning system. Just as private natural-gas suppliers make investment decisions on the basis of such plans, so can suppliers of potable water and liquid-waste systems.

I have already expressed my belief that central governments are the authorities best placed to make strategic decisions about future public infrastructure in their major city-regions. If they can be assisted in such decision-making by an inter-municipal metropolitan planning body, such decisions are likely to be better informed and more politically acceptable to local residents and businesses. But the key point is that there is no reason at all why boundaries of municipalities – even boundaries of multi-functional upper-tier metropolitan or regional authorities – need be determined by the boundaries of water-supply systems and/or sewage-treatment networks. If there is a political will to shape outward urban expansion in particular ways, then regulatory tools combined with judicious decisions by the central government about its own infrastructural investments should be able to do the job. In fact, as we shall see in the next chapter, this is exactly what the Ontario government is now doing in it effort to control urban sprawl in what it calls the Greater Golden Horseshoe.

If urban municipalities are freed from the expectation that they themselves are able to perform specified government functions, then they are also freed from the need to meet any particular requirements about their size. In the past, much attention has been paid to the amalgamation of municipalities. It is now probably time – especially in light of the recent municipal de-amalgamations in Quebec – to pay attention to the conditions under which city residents might be empowered to create smaller municipalities.[6] A minimum condition would have to be that a seceding territory could not leave the remaining municipality in a worse fiscal position than existed before the secession.

The reason for creating the conditions favourable to the creation of smaller municipalities is to reap the benefits that flow from encouraging residents – especially homeowners – to pay very close attention to what is going on within their own municipality. William A. Fischel suggests that, in municipalities with populations of less than 100,000, people hear about what goes on in the municipal council from their neighbours and their own contacts.[7] In municipalities over that size, politics tends to become more like politics at other levels, with the purposes of organized interest groups becoming more important than the expressed views of individual voters.

If municipal secession turns out not be feasible, various forms of political decentralization within large units merit attention. Once again, the situation in the city of Montreal provides an interesting model. Its territory is now divided into nineteen separate boroughs, each of which has its own directly elected mayor and borough council. These councils have the authority to enact local zoning by-laws, provide local services, and even levy a local borough tax on top of the city's tax.[8]

Similar arguments can be made about school boards. In recent decades in Canada, school boards have been first reduced in number and enlarged in territory, and then stripped of much of their original legal authority, especially for taxing local property owners to pay for local schools. All of this has been done in the name of equalizing educational opportunities through various forms of centralized planning and control. But, as with municipalities, the danger now is that few voters will have any direct concerns about the quality of local schools. When schools were locally controlled and at least partly financed by local property-tax payers, then all property owners had a direct stake in the quality of their local school, not only because of their interest in the quality of their children's education, but also because the quality of their local school was an important factor in determining local real-estate values, a subject of huge concern to all property owners.[9]

The recognition that central governments are inevitably going to make key strategic decisions about major infrastructure for public services in city-regions has the effect of widening the options for decision-making at the local level. Specialized bodies can be created to provide certain public services for particular areas, and smaller municipalities and school boards can be encouraged to respond directly and differentially to the many territorially distinct communities that exist within all major city-regions. As long as the central government plays its crucial role, the multiplication of local governments within city-regions will strengthen the capacity of the city-regions to provide innovative solutions to the myriad challenges involved in contemporary urban life.

6

Self-Government for Toronto?

In the first chapter, I noted that, inspired by the ideas of Jane Jacobs, a number of people concerned with Toronto's future – especially Alan Broadbent – have begun a process aimed at creating a self-governing city-region. I have already discussed some of the difficulties in attaining this objective. In my discussion of European city-states, however, I have acknowledged that there is at least one city-region in a Western democracy – Madrid – that seems to possess the kind of institutions that promote a form of genuine urban autonomy. In this chapter, I want to assess the extent to which such autonomy might one day be possible for Toronto. To do this, I must first clarify some of the especially confusing elements of recent debates about Toronto's political status. I will then review recent developments in the province of Ontario's policy-making for urban development in Toronto. Only then can it be determined whether the Madrid model is at all relevant for the governance of the Toronto city-region.

FOUR KINDS OF AUTONOMY FOR TORONTO

There is massive confusion about what it means for Toronto to have more autonomy. There are at least four

senses in which it has been argued in recent years that
Toronto needs more autonomy:

1 *The municipal corporation of the city of Toronto is subject to too
  much detailed day-to-day control by the government of Ontario
  or its agencies.* The point here is that even within its defined
  areas of jurisdiction the municipality cannot do much on its
  own. The best example is land-use planning. Unlike the
  practice in other major cities in North America, all zoning
  decisions in Toronto are subject to appeal to the Ontario
  Municipal Board (OMB) and the grounds for appeal are exceptionally broad. Although provisions of a new City of
  Toronto Act approved by the Ontario legislature in 2006
  loosened some aspects of provincial control, changes to the
  Planning Act did very little to reduce the role of the OMB.
  In terms of its own control over land-use planning, the city
  of Toronto is still a very weak North American urban municipality and there is remarkably little public pressure for
  change. The same rules for land-use planning apply to
  other municipalities in the Toronto city-region.

2 *The municipal corporation of the city of Toronto lacks real autonomy because it has too many functional responsibilities and in-
  sufficient fiscal resources.*[1] Its ability to make effective policy
  decisions on behalf of its citizens is therefore drastically
  limited. The problem can be addressed in two ways: by reducing functional responsibilities and/or by increasing financial resources. Both options have been advanced in the
  literature on this issue. The problem with reducing functional responsibilities is that it would also reduce the ability
  of the municipal corporation to make policy decisions for
  the city of Toronto. But with respect to the city's role in delivering income-security programs (e.g., Ontario Works),

the city has very little autonomy to make policy decisions anyway. Eliminating or reducing the city's obligation to pay 20 per cent of the cost of such programs would, of course, have the effect of increasing its financial resources.

3 *There are some people in the Toronto city-region who still strongly believe that the area needs a form of metropolitan government.* Right now there is no such institution. It appears that the provincial government has filled the vacuum with its own policies related to the "Greenbelt" and "Places to Grow" (more on these below). Although most people concerned with the quality of the urban environment support such policies no matter who makes them, there are some people in municipal-government circles who believe that municipal elected officials should have a direct role in policy-making of this kind and that some form of metropolitan government would be the most appropriate vehicle. This position is not in any way a radical demand for more city-region autonomy. If anything, it is a plea to return to past practices in Ontario, first with the Municipality of Metropolitan Toronto (1954–97) and then with the Greater Toronto Services Board (1998–2001). The province of Ontario has recently established a Greater Toronto Transportation Authority (Metrolinx) covering the territory served by the commuter rail system. Given that the province's recent planning initiatives for the Greater Golden Horseshoe cover a much wider area, it is difficult to imagine a useful metropolitan authority having boundaries that do not include this entire area.

4 *Finally, there is the kind of autonomous Toronto city-region advanced by Alan Broadbent and the signatories of the Greater Toronto Charter.* This approach was discussed in chapter 1 and served as the starting point for the entire book.[2]

The rest of this chapter will primarily be concerned with the fourth option, although some of the discussion will relate to the third as well. Meanwhile, much of the media commentary and public discussion about "more power for Toronto" revolves around the first and second options. My position is similar to that of Jane Jacobs and Alan Broadbent[3] in that I believe that any serious discussion about the governance of cities must begin with the city-region as a whole, not with the central-city municipality, no matter how populous it might be.

THE GOLDEN REPORT

In the mid-1990s, the public debate about the governance of "Greater Toronto" was in fact focused on the city-region as well as on the city of Toronto.[4] In 1995, Anne Golden was appointed by Premier Bob Rae to chair the Task Force on the Future of the Greater Toronto Area. The terms of reference clearly indicated that the task force was concerned with municipal government. The terms stipulated, for example, that the task force should "define a system and a style of governance ... [that] must be founded on a solid base of municipal finance, must promote effective and efficient urban management, must be accountable to and representative of the diverse Toronto of the future, and must promote the broadest civic engagement."[5] The task force was instructed "not to deal with the issue of waste management nor with health management, other than as local services, nor with education governance"[6] because these matters had recently been investigated by other bodies. Most important for our purposes, the territorial ambit of the task force was limited to what was then known as the Greater Toronto Area (GTA)

– the Municipality of Metropolitan Toronto and the regional municipalities of Halton, Peel, York, and Durham. The Office of the Greater Toronto Area had been established within the provincial government since 1988.

The Golden task force was obviously enamoured with *Citistates*, the book by Neal Peirce that attracted a lot of attention in the United States in the early 1990s. It quotes *Citistates* in defining a city-region as being the "'center city, inner and outer suburbs, and rural hinterland ... clearly and intimately interconnected in geography, environment, work force, and [by] a shared economic and social future,'"[7] but states that it defines the GTA in terms of its commutershed, cohesiveness, and anticipated development.[8] There is no discussion in the report, however, of exactly how these criteria were applied. Interestingly a footnote states that "for Jane Jacobs, the city-region is defined by how far its 'economic energy' extends. The city-region emanating from Toronto would correspond to the area we think of as the Golden Horseshoe – the urban area from Niagara to Oshawa with Toronto as its centre."[9]

In the end, the task force avoided making a clear decision about the future boundaries of the new metropolitan government it recommended, stating instead that this task be turned over to an "implementation commission."[10] The very fact that the task force dodged this issue illustrates the difficulty of the boundary issue. But the task force acknowledged this itself when it noted that there was strong support for simply accepting the existing boundaries of the GTA: "In many of our consultations, people argued that no set of boundaries is ideal and that the outcry arising from any proposed changes could obscure and even undermine more important reforms. As well, changes to the region's external boundaries could disrupt existing regional cost-sharing arrangements and necessitate costly restructuring in some areas."[11] It was clear from the task force's discussion of the issue that it largely accepted the GTA boundaries as they were. The only difficult cases involved municipalities on the outer peripheries of Halton, York, and Durham.

The task force recommended that a Greater Toronto Council be established for the GTA and that it be directly responsible for "regional planning; economic development; management of regional assets; and construction and maintenance of expressways."[12] In other words, the new council was to have responsibility for the key strategic decisions relating to the future physical development of the Toronto city-region. This recommendation was never implemented. Instead, the Conservative government of Mike Harris amalgamated the constituent units of the Municipality of Metropolitan Toronto into a new City of Toronto and established the Greater Toronto Services Board (GTSB), which clearly did not have the important direct responsibilities contemplated by the Golden task force. The GTSB turned out to be quite ineffective and was abolished in 2001.

The Liberal provincial government headed by Premier Dalton McGuinty decided to take over responsibility for strategic land-use planning in the GTA. The Golden task force had contemplated such a possibility a decade before but had rejected it, offering this analysis:

> The Task Force believes that, regardless of how the Government of Ontario is structured, it is inherently unable to meet Greater Toronto's coordination needs effectively. The region must develop its own identity and focus as a city-region if it is to compete with other city-regions internationally. The

provincial government, by definition cannot achieve this focus because it defines its constituency Ontario-wide. It also lacks the capacity to advocate freely and effectively on behalf of the city-region, a function that is essential to the GTA's ability to influence federal and provincial policies affecting the region.

... [A] regional coordination function would be both more accountable and less expensive than a provincial one.[13]

Although it is too early to evaluate the effectiveness of the Ontario Liberal government's decision to take over the planning function for the Toronto city-region, it is important to understand its reasoning in so doing. Perhaps its actions indicate some of the reasons why any form of self-government for the Toronto city-region is neither possible nor desirable.

THE GREENBELT AND "PLACES TO GROW"

Soon after coming to office in 2003, the Liberal government of Ontario made it quite clear that it would be taking direct responsibility for land-use planning policy within the Toronto city-region. A year earlier (February 2002), the Progressive Conservative government had appointed a Central Ontario Smart Growth Panel, whose functions were purely advisory. The panel's report formed the basis of much of what the Liberals implemented, although the Liberal approach was more centralized than the plan contemplated by the panel. The territory assigned to the panel for its recommendations was determined by the provincial government. Since the panel's role was purely advisory, most people paid little attention to the boundaries it suggested. These were similar to the boundaries that define what Statistics

Canada refers to as the Extended Golden Horseshoe (the main difference was that the territory covered by the Central Ontario Smart Growth Panel was somewhat larger; Statistics Canada does not include within the horseshoe any of the territory of the cities of Peterborough and Kawartha Lakes and the counties of Peterborough, Haliburton, and Haldimand, and it did not include all of the municipalities within the regions of Niagara and Waterloo or the counties of Wellington, Dufferin, and Simcoe).

Larry Bourne, one of Canada's foremost urban geographers, has pointed out that the construction of the Central Ontario Zone corresponds to no known geographical principles:

> The building blocks used to define the region – the old counties – are in many instances no longer useful as geographical containers. Nor is it a "functional region" in the sense that it is based on integration or linkage criteria, such as the daily journey to work (used to delimit the CMAS) or weekly recreational travel (often called the urban field). Nor does it represent the service hinterland of Toronto or of the other urban nodes. It also incorporates distinctively different physical and socio-economic landscapes. As an additional reservation, only limited data sources and almost no analytical studies cover the Central Ontario Zone. Thus, there is no accumulated history of empirical research or policy studies.[14]

Bourne also points out that the zone contains nine separate urban nodes: Toronto, Hamilton, Oshawa, Kitchener-Waterloo, St Catharines–Niagara, Peterborough, Guelph, Barrie, and Brantford. These are contained within four distinct subzones:

1 The urbanized core, which includes Toronto, Oshawa, and Hamilton CMAS

2 The newer and smaller suburban and ex-urban communities immediately surrounding these CMAS

3 Other metropolitan areas and smaller urban centres, including Kitchener-Waterloo, St Catharines–Niagara, Guelph, Barrie, and Peterborough

4 The hinterland, "that part of the Central Ontario Zone that is not heavily urbanized and indeed may not be tightly integrated with any of the urbanized cores in the Zone"[15]

Whatever its virtues for the purposes of large-scale regional planning, it is scarcely surprising that the Central Ontario Zone evokes no feelings of regional or political attachment among its residents.[16]

In 2003, the Liberal government adopted the same territory (minus the county of Haliburton) for its planning initiative in the Toronto city-region, but started calling it the Greater Golden Horseshoe (GGH). (See Map 4, page 19.) One of the most remarkable features of the Liberal policy was that its definition of the GGH received virtually no public attention. Had the Liberals been establishing a new form of metropolitan government with such boundaries, this could not possibly have been the case. But who in Ontario ever gets excited about how the provincial government organizes itself territorially for its own purposes?

These boundaries have turned out to be of immense significance, especially for large property owners. The newly established Greenbelt is all well within the GGH, and much of it had already been protected by other provincial legislation.[17] Much more significant is the Places to Grow Act, which was approved by the Ontario legislature in 2005. This legislation gives an Ontario cabinet minister the authority to establish "growth plans" for designated areas in Ontario. Such plans establish the basic rules of municipal land-use planning within that territory. The growth plan for the Greater Golden Horseshoe was promulgated by the Ontario government in June 2006.[18] It lays down elaborate rules by which the anticipated 3.7 million new residents in the GGH will be accommodated between implementation of the plan (2006) and 2031. The main theme of the plan is intensification. By the year 2015, 40 per cent of all new residential development in each single- and upper-tier municipality will be required to take place within established built-up areas. Meanwhile, there will also be specific intensification targets for both jobs and residents within designated growth centres and new greenfield developments.

At least until adjacent areas of the province receive their own growth plans from the Ontario government, lands within the GGH will be subject to different planning constraints from those just outside it. A planner for the city of Brantford has recently outlined some of the problems this poses for his municipality. First, the designated density target within the downtown area is 150 residents and jobs per hectare, while the current density is only about 100. In counting residents and jobs, the city is not permitted to count post-secondary students in residences or jobs in entertainment facilities. The same planner has also pointed out that while municipalities can control the density of development for industrial development, they have no control over the number of jobs within each building. Because of its location, Brantford is attractive in logistical terms, appealing to warehouse operations that have small numbers of jobs but large buildings. Meanwhile, the city of Woodstock, about sixty kilometres to the northwest, is just outside the boundaries of the GGH. It is experiencing a boom in industrial development – especially because of the development of a new Toyota plant – but is not subject to the intensification requirements of the Places to Grow Act. Understandably, there is some feeling in Brantford that the rules of the game are simply not fair.[19]

In a very real way, the government of Ontario is now acting as the strategic planning authority for the territory of a city-region it calls the Greater Golden Horseshoe. There is virtually no awareness among the general public that such a territorial entity even exists. Its boundaries were established without any public discussion or debate. The land-use policies that have been announced for this area have attracted the attention of developers, environmentalists, and municipal officials, but there has been virtually no public controversy about them – which is remarkable given the explicit aim of the policy to intensify urban development throughout the territory of the GGH. It is easy to imagine how different things would have been if the provincial government had in 2003 announced plans to establish a GGH council comprised of directly elected members or municipal delegates, and stated that it would ask such a council to develop a plan to accommodate 3.7 million new residents over twenty-five years. We would probably still be debating the potential territorial boundaries of the new GGH, and feelings would be running high in peripheral communities about whether they would gain or lose from being included. Mobilizing majority support for intensification within such a council would not have been an easy task.

If we assume that the GGH growth plan was designed to further the best interests of the Toronto city-region, we must explain why the Golden task force appears to have been so dramatically wrong in assuming that the "provincial government, by definition cannot achieve this focus because it defines its constituency Ontario-wide." My explanation is simple: any Ontario-wide perspective on infrastructure and the built environment must of necessity focus on a territory that roughly matches the territory of the GGH. Such a territory already is home to more than half the population of Ontario, and it is the expected location of almost all future population growth.

But what allows the provincial legislature – dominated as it is by members from the GGH – to make decisions that likely could not have been made elsewhere? There are a few reasons. First, because the boundaries of the GGH did not relate to any new institutions (proclaiming the GGH growth plan required no decisions about institutions, though decisions about boundaries were required) and had no any immediate impact on the everyday life of residents, they attracted almost no media or public scrutiny. Second, the decision to pursue the GGH growth plan was clearly made at the highest levels of the Liberal government – that is, by the premier and his cabinet. Because Ontario operates within a parliamentary system (unlike non-partisan municipal councils), once the decision was made, it could not be overturned, because the Liberals held a majority within the legislature. In any event, "doing something about sprawl" was in theory politically attractive. It will take a few years before the policy translates into building particular high-density developments in opposition to the wishes of nearby residents. The real test for the policy will be the extent to which it survives such opposition. This is why it is far too early to decide whether the policy is effective or not. My claim is only that the policy would not even have been agreed to – let alone implemented – had its subject matter been delegated to some new "local" authority especially established to govern the GGH.

The provincial adoption of an anti-sprawl policy explains why there have been no public claims by anyone – including anyone who once advocated for a more autonomous Toronto city-region – that the government of Ontario has been trampling on local autonomy or on the potential for city-region autonomy. The people who had advocated for more autonomy for the Toronto city-region are generally the same ones who are now most supportive of strong anti-sprawl policies. Because the province is delivering on such policies, they seem content. At some point, we might well hear objections from residents and businesses in places such as Brantford, but right now the issues are too obscure and complicated to receive much attention in the political sphere.

THE MADRID EXAMPLE

If the Greater Golden Horseshoe were to become a Canadian province in the way that Madrid in Spain is an autonomous community, there would have to be separate provinces for eastern and western Ontario as well, because the two areas are separated from each other by the territory of the GGH. Northern Ontario would then presumably also become a province. This is not going to happen.

Nevertheless, it is worth speculating about what the politics of a GGH province would look like. The first point is that there would likely be considerable tension between the city of Toronto and the rest of the GGH. This is because the city would make up more than a third of the total population, not enough to control the politics of the GGH but probably enough to ensure that the non-city areas would often unite politically to prevent city dominance. This would be bad news for those who see an autonomous city-region as a force that would act in favour of the interests of the central city. The second point is that we can assume that the GGH province would be governed by a partisan legislature and a parliamentary government. We would be wrong to envision its governmental institutions as being like those of municipalities writ large. There would be no particular reason to expect the partisan makeup of a GGH province to be much different from that of the rest of Ontario. More than half of Ontario's electoral districts are within the GGH, including many that have significant rural and small-town components. In the 2007 Ontario election, the Liberal Party dominated in the GGH (winning 45 of 68 electoral districts), just as it did in the province as a whole (71 of 107 electoral districts).

Ironically, one of the more likely outcomes could well be that a GGH provincial government would have greater difficulty imposing the kinds of tough planning policies associated with the Places to Grow Act than a municipal council would. Just as non-partisan majorities on municipal councils find it difficult to agree to and enforce intensification policies in cases where citizens object, it could be equally difficult for a partisan GGH majority to do the same thing. All GGH legislators would have an intense interest in matters of urban development, regardless of their party affiliation. Under the current regime in Ontario, the Places to Grow legislation provides a framework by which a designated minister can promulgate growth plans for any area in the province, the first area – because it is the most important – being the GGH. If the GGH were itself a province, it is surely much less likely that the legislature would agree to place the entire GGH growth plans in the hands of the minister. This is simply another way of saying that desirable urban policies will not necessarily emerge from legislatures that are primarily concerned with urban issues. Perhaps a more hospitable environment would be one in which the legislature were somewhat removed from such policies; in which the premier – whose personal political base may lie somewhere other than in the GGH (in Ottawa in the case of Premier Dalton McGuinty) – is strongly committed; and in which the provincial bureaucracy had the requisite knowledge and relevant technical skills to develop a policy that could work. Besides, any attempt to impose restrictive planning policies within the GGH might simply encourage developers to move outside the boundaries to the new provinces in western and eastern Ontario. In a single Ontario province, steps can be taken at the provincial level to make such behaviour less likely, but where there might be three provinces, interprovincial cooperation on this kind of issue could be difficult.

Precisely because Toronto is a growing and dynamic city-region, it would be exceptionally difficult to reach a useful political agreement about its appropriate boundaries for the purposes of self-government. Madrid is not so dynamic and explosive in its economic growth. More relevant to real-world politics is the fact that, in the aftermath of Franco's dictatorship and in an environment in which Catalans, Basques, and Galicians were pressing for regional autonomy, the entire territorial basis of the Spanish state had to be restructured. As a by-product of this process, the Madrid city-region acquired its own "autonomous community." It is conceivable that one day a territorially truncated Canadian state will have to restructure itself in a similar way; that Ontario will have to be divided; and that a by-product might be something that looks like a province for Toronto. If this ever happens, it will not be the result of a search for more effective urban governance. It will be the result of the powerful and sustained force of Quebec nationalism, just as self-governance for Madrid was the result of region-based nationalism elsewhere in Spain.

Conclusion

I emphasized at the end of chapter 1 that there is no reason
why the increasing importance of cities as sources of economic
growth and innovation necessarily leads to the increased importance of municipalities or the decreased importance of central governments. Instead, I pointed to the likelihood that
central governments would become *more* involved in major issues relating to urban growth and development than they
have been in the past. The discussion in chapter 6 of the current policies of the government of Ontario with respect to
Toronto's Greater Golden Horseshoe is an important example. How should those of us concerned with the democratic
governance of our city-regions respond?

The temptation, of course, is to focus on the need for institutional change. This is exactly the course of action chosen
by the authors of the Greater Toronto Charter and described
in chapter 1. The charter was developed by experienced,
thoughtful citizens who are passionately concerned about
Toronto's urban future. This is reason enough for Canadian
academics to pay attention. But there are also two other reasons: (1) the charter was directly inspired by the work of
Jane Jacobs, probably the most influential urban thinker of

the twentieth century; and (2) although the charter might seem
politically naive, it encapsulates in the clearest terms possible
much of the current future-oriented thinking about city governance. Each of these reasons deserves further consideration.

The reason the work of Jane Jacobs has been so influential
is because she understood how central cities work. In particular, she instinctively knew that fine-grained, mixed uses of
land are essential for successful neighbourhoods and that
central cities breed economic innovation by making it possible for all kinds of synergetic economic activities to exist in
close proximity to each other. Her greatest books, *The Death
and Life of Great American Cities* and *The Economy of Cities*, are
devoted to each of these arguments respectively. *Cities and the
Wealth of Nations* is not about central cities; it is about the
economies of city-regions and the allegedly harmful role of
central governments (national or sub-national) in shaping
their development. It is this book that was most relevant to
the authors of the Greater Toronto Charter, and even to those
who later invoked her name in simply demanding more legislative and financial autonomy for central-city municipal
governments. Unfortunately, it is this book, among the three,
that is the most flawed. City-region currencies were essential
to her vision, but she never worked out how they could dis-
place national currencies, let alone international ones like the
Euro. Because she had little use for large corporations, she ignored the problems that the creation of hundreds of new currencies would cause for such corporations. And with regard
to a point I have emphasized throughout this book, she also
ignored the problem of determining the boundaries within
which each of these currencies would be legal tender.

It would obviously be wrong to attribute to *Cities and the
Wealth of Nations* the fact that, since its publication in 1984,

there has been so much international attention paid to the rise of "global cities." But Jacobs's work clearly played an important role, even if some academics do not always acknowledge her influence.[1] As I have repeatedly tried to show, global-city scholars have paid scarcely any attention to the governance of global cities, and even less to their formal governmental structures. Other scholars, such as Warren Magnusson and Gerald Frug, who have been explicitly concerned with thinking about new ways of conceiving city-region governance have paid scant attention to boundaries. Well-known consultants and popularizers, such as Neal Peirce, have simply been vague.

All this has led to the widely held belief that the governmental institutions of city-regions have to somehow catch up with the growing importance of urban economies. Such a belief is not just a variant on long-standing debates about the relationship between politics and economics. It is more a debate about scale; it is a claim that central governments are simply incapable of responding to the economic and social needs of city-regions. This is the claim that lies at the heart of the Greater Toronto Charter.

As I have attempted to argue throughout this book, the core problem with this approach is that city-regions are wrongly conceived as specified territories that can be established with institutions of government that are analogous to those of nation-states or provinces. City-regions cannot be defined territorially in the same way as these other levels of authority. The virtues of the boundaries of nation-states and provinces are precisely that they usually are "artificial" and that when they are successful – which has been increasingly the case in recent decades – they are quite uncontested. The very act of thinking about the boundaries of city-regions involves thinking about rational ways of constructing them, in the same way that the descendants of Charlemagne were supposed to divide up Europe according to the Treaty of Verdun in 843. But this book has identified multiple criteria for drawing city-region boundaries, each of which leads to different results and each of which will always be changing. Earlier chapters have also pointed to important political reasons why inhabitants of different areas within city-regions are unlikely to agree with one another on common boundaries.

The authors of the Greater Toronto Charter – and all those who advocate forms of self-governance for city-regions – are engaged in an impossible task. Their apparent objective is noble, but the enterprise is conceptually flawed. Their real objective, of course, is to enhance the quality of our collective lives, even if they do have some difficulty (as we all do) in defining the relevant collectivity. Fortunately, in most parts of the democratic world, certainly in Canada, we have multiple layers of government and multiple forms of governmental authorities that can respond to different kinds of urban problems at different scales. We need not redesign the ways in which our city-regions are governed; rather we need to make better use of the wide array of institutions that we already have. We need be just as concerned about institutional arrangements for small-scale issues in our cities as we are about large-scale issues.

In its 2006 report, the External Advisory Committee on Cities and Communities, (chaired by Michael Harcourt, former mayor of Vancouver and former premier of British Columbia) comes to conclusions that closely resemble the main thesis of this book. After making all the common arguments about the importance of cities and their regions, the report states that the committee was persuaded by arguments for greater local autonomy and integrated approaches in policy-making. Regional governments in the OECD, similar in scale to Canadian provinces and territories, have crucial strategic roles in selecting priorities for places, policies and programs. Intercity networks, city-region effects and city-to-rural connections are valuable aspects of development that are less than national in scope and more than municipal in their functioning.[2]

The report continues: "[P]rovinces and territories [must] in turn ... devolve clear tasks and resources to municipalities."[3] It does not state precisely what those tasks and resources should be, and neither have I focused on this issue in this book, except to point out that many important local public services (e.g., schools and hospitals) are not municipal responsibilities in Canada and are unlikely to become so in the foreseeable future. In any event, there are many ways to provide local services, and direct municipal provision is just one of them. If we insist that municipalities have clear and direct responsibility for a wide range of services that are crucial to the well-being of our city-regions, we are likely to create municipalities that are too large to effectively look after the thousands of details of urban life that are cumulatively so important.

What about central-city municipalities? Should they have a kind of special status within provinces? Certainly this is the case that the city of Toronto made with partial success to the government of Ontario. But Ontario has now extended much of Toronto's new authority to most other Ontario municipalities. It is true that some American central-city municipalities (notably New York City) have functional and taxing authorities that other municipalities within the same state lack. It is well known, however, that the stories of most American central cities in recent decades have not been happy, even if there are some recent signs of renewal. The levying of a municipal income tax on all workers in the municipality is one of the causes (but clearly not the only one) of the migration of jobs to suburban municipalities. It seems that there can be as many problems as benefits when municipalities have the right to levy such a tax. The same can be said of municipal sales taxes.

Debates and conflicts about the relative role of the provincial government on the one hand and that of municipalities and other local authorities (e.g., school boards) on the other are endemic to provincial-local relations. There will never be a definitive answer about "Who does what?" We need strong municipalities and local authorities involved in a great variety of public services, and we need strong provincial governments that lay down the general policies and ensure that they are not violated.

As we have seen throughout this book, Canadian provinces are the kind of intermediate mechanisms between the national state and the local municipality that other countries sorely lack or have only recently created. Perhaps because provinces have been with us for so long and have had ample opportunity to err and to annoy, they are (outside Quebec and perhaps Alberta and British Columbia) often seen as the level of government we can do without. As globalization spurs economic activity in our growing city-regions and sucks people off the land and out of resource-based communities, there is a certain logic to the claim that provinces are outmoded. After all, when the provinces joined Canada, their primary functions related to resources and agriculture. It is not obvious that they are now in the process of becoming the much-needed governments of our city-regions, especially when they still include such immense expanses of lakes, rocks, and trees within their boundaries.

Finding appropriate institutions for the governance of the world's city-regions is rightly a priority for a great many governments and researchers throughout the developed world. Because we have accepted for so long that sovereign states (and their constituent units within federations) have clear and stable boundaries, it is understandable why some would think that we can define similar boundaries for city-regions in such a way that city-regions, as institutions of government, can somehow replace the outmoded institutions that emerged to deal with different problems in previous centuries.

City-regions are different from sovereign states (and their constituent units, if any) because their importance is intimately connected to the fact that they have different boundaries for different purposes and that these multiple boundaries are themselves constantly in flux and usually expanding. Such a state of affairs provides ample theoretical and empirical opportunity for social scientists to analyse and to measure. But practical politicians, who must build and nurture the institutions that make our relatively safe and comfortable lives possible, require more. They need to know where the ambit of one institution of government ends and where another one begins. In short, they need boundaries. Because we cannot draw stable multi-purpose boundaries for city-regions, we are incapable of designing the institutions that are needed for city-regions to be self-governing.

⎿→ WHAT ABOUT RURAL?

Notes

CHAPTER ONE

1 For a full, critical discussion, see Krasner, *Sovereignty*.

2 However, since Hong Kong and Macau were absorbed into the People's Republic of China in 1997, China has proven that it is possible for a single sovereign state to have different legal currencies in different territories.

3 But see Sancton, "Jane Jacobs."

4 For her thoughts on large organizations vs small organizations, see Jacobs, *Canadian Cities and Sovereignty Association*, 31–5.

5 Jacobs, *Cities and the Wealth of Nations*, 45.

6 Ibid., 47.

7 Ibid., 45.

8 Ibid., 57.

9 Ibid., 169. After independence, Singapore briefly shared a currency with Malaysia. For a brief account of how and why this arrangement broke down, see Helleiner, *The Making of National Money*, 206–8.

10 Hill and Fujita, "The Nested City," 215.

11 Bunnell, Muzaini, and Sidaway, "Global City Frontiers."

12 Kresl and Fry, *The Urban Response*, 153–4.

13 Jacobs, *Cities and the Wealth of Nations,* 174.

14 Ironically, the Dutch currency is now most famous for its role in relation to the "Dutch disease" of the 1960s, when revenue from North Sea oil caused its dramatic appreciation in value, thereby harming Dutch manufacturing. The subsequent adoption of the Euro might well have deprived the Dutch ring city of an accurate economic feedback mechanism, but it also has protected it from faulty local feedback of the kind provided by North Sea oil, the extraction of which had little to do with wealth creation in cities. For a brief discussion of the Dutch disease, see Ebrahim-zadeh, "Back to Basics."

15 Rowe, "Editor's Notes," 2.

16 "The Greater Toronto Charter," in Broadbent et al., *Towards a New City of Toronto Act,* 40.

17 Broadbent, "The Place of Cities," 3.

18 Broadbent. "A New Canada," 24.

19 Broadbent, "Introduction," 6.

20 Stevenson, "Possible Regional Implications," 28.

21 There was another layer of confusion as well. While Broadbent and Stevenson were writing in a collection entitled *Towards a New City of Toronto Act,* the province of Ontario and the city of Toronto were negotiating about a new statutory framework for the city (the City of Toronto Act). These negotiations had nothing whatever to do with governmental arrangements for any geographical version of a larger Toronto region.

22 Broadbent, *Urban Nation,* 201.

23 Ibid., 124.

24 Ibid., 202–5

25 Ibid., 205.

26 I have discussed this debate in my book *Merger Mania,* especially chap. 3.

27 More than twenty years ago, we collaborated as joint editors on *City Politics in Canada*.

28 Frug, *City Making*, 214–15.

29 Ibid., 85–6.

30 Ibid., 87.

31 Ibid., 88.

32 Ibid., 217.

33 Ibid., 245n8.

34 Magnusson, *The Search*, 55–6.

35 Sassen, *The Global City.*

36 Ward, "The Successful Management," 299–300.

37 Ohmae, *End of the Nation State*, 97, 100.

38 Ibid., 136–8.

39 Peirce, *Citistates*, ix.

40 Ibid., 8.

41 Ibid., 13.

42 Michael Bliss has recently added his contribution: "Perhaps Canadians may continue to prosper and enjoy the good life as the country evolves into a league of provinces, and perhaps a sprinkling of city-states, some of these jurisdictions effectively independent, some interested in joining the United States." Bliss, "Has Canada Failed?" 5.

CHAPTER TWO

1 Dahl, "The City," 954.

2 Alesina and Spolaore, *The Size of Nations*, 3.

3 Ibid.

4 Ibid., 4–5.

5 For another account of such a method of governmental organization, see the description by Hooghe and Marks of what they call "Type 2 governance" in "Unraveling the Central State," 237–9.

6 Alesina and Spolaore, *The Size of Nations*, 23.

7 Ibid., 23.

8 Ibid., 15.

9 Ibid., 81, 219.

10 Ibid., 207.

11 Ibid., 137.

12 Ibid., 5.

13 Ibid., 4.

14 Planhol, *An Historical Geography of France*, 91.

15 Ibid., 92.

16 Ibid., 93.

17 This book does not treat the city-states of the Persian Gulf, in large measure because they generally do not qualify as liberal democracies, but Kuwait, Bahrain, and Qatar are sovereign city-states and Abu Dhabi and Dubai are city-states within the federation that is the United Arab Emirates.

18 The literature on the emergence of sovereign states in Europe is huge. Like Sassen in *Territory Authority· Rights*, I shall follow Spruyt's account in *The Sovereign State.*

19 Spruyt, *The Sovereign State*, 128.

20 Ibid., 67.

21 Ibid., 147.

22 Ibid., 148.

23 Chapman, *The Congress of Vienna*, 41.

24 As quoted in Margaret Macmillan, *Paris 1919*, 12.

25 Judt, *Postwar.*

26 For a powerful argument that the rigidity of the post-colonial boundaries of African sovereign states is one of the continent's fundamental problems, see Herbst, *States and Power.*

27 Anderson, *Frontiers*, 86–7.

28 For an excellent recent survey of political issues relating to national boundaries in various parts of the world, see O'Leary, Lustick, and Callaghy, eds, *Right-sizing the State.*

29 "All successful and many attempted secessions in the twentieth century involved federal units or political units which had their own legislatures and executive governments prior to secession … [S]ince the borders of these units have already been marked, the new authorities simply transformed these internal borders into inter-state borders." Pavkovic and Radan, *Creating New States*, 13–14.

30 Taylor, "World Cities," 58.

31 Ibid., 59.

32 Jackson, "Sovereignty and Its Presuppositions," 297.

33 Buchanan, "The Making and Unmaking of Boundaries," 231.

34 Ibid., 236.

35 Planhol, *An Historical Geography of France*, 281.

36 Ibid., 281–2.

37 Ibid., 283.

38 Loughlin, *Subnational Government*, esp. 110–17.

39 National Geographic Society, *Historical Atlas*, 106.

40 Peters, "Manhattan."

41 Public Policy Institute, *Could New York Let Upstate Be Upstate?*

42 In 1999, as a result of an act of the Parliament of Canada, the new territory of Nunavut was created. Because all of its territory came from the Northwest Territories, Nunavut's creation did not affect any Canadian provincial boundaries.

43 Maritime Union Study, *The Report on Maritime Union*. Since 1970, there has been more discussion of splitting the Maritime provinces than of uniting them. The Parti acadien in New Brunswick advocated a separate province for Acadians in the 1980s. See Gauvin and Jalbert, "The Rise and Fall of the Parti Acadien." In 2003, the Cape Breton Regional Municipality commissioned a study on different political options for Cape Breton, including separation from Nova Scotia. See Locke and Tomblin, *Good Governance*.

44 Young, *Secession of Quebec*, 213–15.

45 Emery and Kneebone, *Should Alberta and Saskatchewan Unite?* 22.
46 Di Matteo, Emery, and English, "Is It Better to Live in a Basement?"
47 Anderson, *Frontiers*, 48–51.
48 Gunlicks, *The Länder*, 200.
49 Leonardy, "Territorial Reform," 66.
50 Gunlicks, *The Länder*, 36–43.
51 Keating, Loughlin, and Deschouwer, *Culture, Institutions, and Economic Development*, 41–3.
52 Ibid., 75–80.

CHAPTER THREE

1 See the discussion at the beginning of chapter 2.
2 Hooghe and Marks, "Unraveling the Central State," 237–9.
3 Burns, *Formation of American Local Governments*.
4 The definitive account of the New York consolidation is in Harmack, *Power and Society*.
5 For a comprehensive and historical account of regional planning for city-regions, especially in the British context, see Hall, *Theory and Practice of Regional Planning*.
6 Travers, *Politics of London*.
7 Sancton, *Merger Mania*, 113–40.
8 L.J. Sharpe, ed., *Government of World Cities*.
9 Brownstone and Plunkett, *Metropolitan Winnipeg*.
10 There is a large and burgeoning literature on this topic. For major studies, see Sellers, *Governing from Below*, and Brenner, *New State Spaces*.
11 Savitch and Vogel, "Suburbs without a City."
12 Frug, *City Making*, 245n8.
13 Travers, *Politics of London*, 3.
14 For a recent comprehensive account of various methods of mapping city-regions in England, see Robson et al., "Mapping City-Regions."

15 Murphy, *Preliminary 2006 ... Delineation*, Appendix A.

16 For a recent discussion of "What constitutes the New York and Los Angeles metropolises?" see Beveridge and Weber, "Race and Class," 50–3.

17 United States, "Standards for Defining."

18 United States, *OMB Bulletin*, 22 February 2005.

19 Frug's proposal is discussed in more detail in chapter 1.

20 Quebec, Task Force on Greater Montreal, *Montreal*, 15.

21 Quebec, *Pacte 2000*, 277.

22 Quebec, l'Assemblée nationale, *Débats*, 6 June 2000.

23 Quebec, *Statutes of Quebec 2000*, chap. 56, s. 66–7.

24 Quebec, *Statutes of Quebec 2001*, chap. 68, s. 107.

25 Calculated from data in the *2006 Census of Canada* available on the Statistics Canada website.

26 Masson, *Alberta's Local Governments*, 164–6.

27 Calgary, "Annexation Frequently Asked Questions," no. 3.

28 For a brief account of Calgary's absorption of the municipalities of Bowness, Montgomery, and the hamlet of Forest Lawn (total population, 14,000) in the early 1960s, see Parker, "Calgary," 29–30.

CHAPTER FOUR

1 For a comprehensive introduction, see Buchanan and Moore, eds, *States, Nations, and Borders*. For a political approach to economic analyses of secession, see Young, "Secession as Revolution."

2 Wellman, *A Theory of Secession*, 62–3.

3 Ibid., 36.

4 Ibid., 58–9.

5 Magnusson, *Search for Political Space*. For a brief discussion of Magnusson's approach, see chapter 1 of this book.

6 Wellman, *A Theory of Secession*, 32.

7 Ibid., 184.

8 Sonenshein, *City at Stake*; and Faught, "Breaking Up Is Hard to Do."

9 Young, "Secession as Revolution, " 374.

10 Frug, *City Making*. For a discussion of Frug's approach, see chapter 1 of this book.

11 Mayor Mel Lastman of Toronto expressed support for such a possibility in 1999. See Boudreau, "Intergovernmental Relations," 169–70; and Toronto, "Powers of Canadian Cities, " 9.

12 This is one of those rare occasions where Wikipedia is the only possible source, because someone carefully made these calculations in the "Province of Toronto" entry. Even here, however, there is some uncertainty about what territory this new province should encompass. Interested readers should also consult the "Discussion" section of the entry, where participants debate the seriousness of the "Province of Toronto" campaign. For Wikipedia, see http://en.wikipedia.org/wiki/Province_of_Toronto. For the "Province of Toronto" website, see www.provinceoftoronto.ca/. Both websites accessed 20 June 2007.

13 See chapter 1 for brief discussions of these authors.

14 L.J. Sharpe, "The Failure of Local Government Modernization," 97.

15 Leonardy, "Territorial Reform, " 72–3.

16 Gunlicks, *The Länder and German Federalism*, 103.

17 Herrschel and Newman, "Global Competition, " 208. See also Kresl, *Planning*, 133.

18 Herrschel and Newman, "Global Competition, " 208.

19 Parker, *Sovereign City*, 206.

20 Blatter, "Geographic Scale, " 129.

21 Herrschel and Newman, "Global Competition, " 211.

22 Blatter, "Geographic Scale, " 127.

23 Ibid., 130.

24 Ibid.

25 Herrschel and Newman, *Governance of Europe's City-Regions*, 159.
26 Haussermann, "Berlin."
27 Herrschel and Newman, *Governance of Europe's City-Regions*, 163–4.
28 Gunlicks, *The* Länder, 105.
29 Herrschel and Newman, *Governance of Europe's City-Regions*, 167.
30 Bullman, "Austria, " 120.
31 Paal, "Metropolitan Governance ... in Vienna, " 235.
32 Schwab and Kubler, "Metropolitan Governance, " 23.
33 For a brief discussion of issues concerning metropolitan governance in Brussels prior to and after 1989, see Ternhorst and van de Ven, "Territorialisation of the State, " 417–25.
34 Its status under various constitutional hypotheses is much debated. See Dumont and Van Drooghenbroeck, "The Status of Brussels."
35 Lagrou, "Brussels, " 313.
36 Ibid.
37 Ibid.
38 Ibid., 315–16.
39 Herrschel and Newman, *Governance of Europe's City-Regions*, 97.
40 Maldonado, "Metropolitan Government ... in Madrid, " 360.
41 Ibid.
42 Ibid.
43 Ibid., 363.

CHAPTER FIVE

1 For the classic analysis of Britain and France, see Ashford, *British Dogmatism*. See also Keating, *Comparative Urban Politics*.
2 Canada, *2006 Census of Canada*. www12.statcan.ca/english/census06/data/popdwell/Table.cfm?T=601&PR=13&S=0&O=A&RPP=25 (accessed 22 June 2007).

3 For details, see Sancton, *Merger Mania*, 36–40, 70–4.

4 Quebec, *Pacte 2000*, 292.

5 The Vancouver Board of Parks and Recreation, comprising seven directly elected members, is an exception. See http:// vancouver.ca/parks/ (accessed 22 June 2007).

6 Fischel, *The Homevoter Hypothesis*, 285–7.

7 Ibid., chap. 4.

8 Sancton, "Fusions et défusions municipales." This paper is available in English at www.cpsa-acsp.ca/papers-2006/Sancton.pdf (accessed 22 June 2007).

9 Fischel, *The Homevoter Hypothesis*, chap. 6.

CHAPTER SIX

1 The most recent item is Courchene, "Global Futures for Canada's Global Cities."

2 For an earlier effort to clarify some of the confusion, see Keil and Young, "A Charter for the People?"

3 As noted in chapter 1, Broadbent's position changed somewhat in 2008 with the publication of his *Urban Nation*. In this book he suggests that self-governing city-regions would do well initially to adopt boundaries that correspond to those of the central-city municipality, in the expectation that neighbouring cities would then opt in voluntarily.

4 For a comprehensive account of the historical background prior to this, see Frisken, *Public Metropolis*, and White, *Growth Plan*.

5 Ontario, *Greater Toronto*, 229.

6 Ibid., 232.

7 Ibid., 23.

8 Ibid., 24.

9 Ibid., 23.

10 Ibid., 169.

11 Ibid., 166.

12 Ibid., 184.

13 Ibid., 163.

14 Bourne, *Social Change in the Central Ontario Region*, 7–8.

15 Ibid., 9.

16 Richard Florida has developed an even more territorially expansive version of the Toronto "mega-region." He claims that it stretches from "from Waterloo, and London, Ontario, through Toronto eastward to Ottawa, Montreal, and Quebec City and down to Syracuse, Ithaca, and Utica in the United States." Although he refers to this mega-region as being "bi-national" (United States and Canada), he makes no other reference to Quebec in the entire book, except to note that "Montreal is home to Cirque de Soleil and a world-class music scene that produced the Arcade Fire, one of the leading and most successful bands of the early 2000s." See his *Who's Your City*, 52–3.

17 Ontario, Municipal Affairs and Housing, *Greenbelt Plan 2005*.

18 Ontario, Public Infrastructure Renewal, *Growth Plan ... 2006*.

19 Reniers, "Implementing."

CONCLUSION

1 Exceptions are Andrew E.G. Jonas and Kevin Ward: "Arguably, one of the most prescient analyses of present possibilities [of city-regions] can be found in Jane Jacobs' writings, especially her polemic on *Cities and the Wealth of Nations* ... Therein Jacobs laid out a powerful argument to the effect that cities rather than nations are agents of wealth creation." See their "Introduction to a Debate on City-Regions," 171.

2 Canada, Infrastructure Canada, *From Restless Communities*, 22.

3 Ibid.

Bibliography

Alesina, Alberto, and Enrico Spolaore. *The Size of Nations.* Cambridge: MIT Press, 2003

Anderson, Malcolm. *Frontiers: Territory and State Formation in the Modern World.* Cambridge, UK: Polity Press, 1996

Ashford, Douglas E. *British Dogmatism and French Pragmatism: Central-Local Policy-Making in the Welfare State.* London: George Allen & Unwin, 1982

Beveridge, Andrew A., and Susan Weber. "Race and Class in the Developing New York and Los Angeles Metropolises." In *New York and Los Angeles: Politics, Society, and Culture, A Comparative View,* edited by David Halle, 49–78. Chicago: University of Chicago Press, 2003

Blatter, Joachim. "Geographic Scale and Functional Scope in Metropolitan Governance Reform: Theory and Evidence from Germany." *Journal of Urban Affairs* 28, no. 2 (2006): 121–50

Bliss, Michael. "Has Canada Failed?" *Literary Review of Canada* 14, no. 2 (March 2006)

Boudreau, Julie-Anne. "Intergovernmental Relations and Polyscalar Social Mobilization: The Cases of Montreal and Toronto." In *Canada: The State of the Federation 2004 – Municipal-Federal-Provincial Relations in Canada,* edited by Robert Young and Christian Leuprecht, 161–80. Montreal and Kingston: McGill-Queen's University Press, 2006

Bourne, Larry. *Social Change in the Central Ontario Region*. Issue paper no. 8. Toronto: Neptis Foundation for the Ontario Smart Growth Panel, 2003

Brenner, Neil. *New State Spaces: Urban Governance and the Rescaling of Statehood*. New York: Oxford University Press, 2004

Broadbent, Alan. "The Place of Cities in Canada: Inside the Constitutional Box and Out." *Caledon Commentary*, June 2002, 1–6

– "A New Canada for the 21st Century." *Ideas That Matter* 3, no. 1 (2003): 21–5

– "Introduction." In Broadbent et al., *Towards a New City of Toronto Act*, 5–9

– *Urban Nation: Why We Need to Give Power back to the Cities to Make Canada Strong*. Toronto: HarperCollins 2008

Broadbent, Alan, et al. *Towards a New City of Toronto Act*. Toronto: Zephyr Press, 2005

Brownstone, Meyer, and T.J. Plunkett. *Metropolitan Winnipeg: Politics and Reform of Local Government*. Berkeley: University of California Press, 1983

Buchanan, Allen. "The Making and Unmaking of Boundaries: What Liberalism Has to Say." In Buchanan and Moore, *States, Nations, and Borders*, 231–61

Buchanan, Allen, and Margaret Moore, eds. *States, Nations, and Borders: The Ethics of Making Boundaries*. Cambridge, UK: Cambridge University Press, 2003

Bullman, Udo. "Austria: The End of Proportional Government." In *Subnational Democracy in the European Union: Challenges and Changes*, edited by John Loughlin, 117–42. Oxford: Oxford University Press, 2001

Bunnell, T., H.B. Muzaini, and J.D. Sidaway. "Global City Frontiers: Singapore's Hinterland and the Contested Socio-Political Geographies of Bintan." *International Journal of Urban and Regional Research* 30, no. 1 (2006): 3–22

Bibliography 153

Burns, Nancy. *The Formation of American Local Governments: Private Values in Public Institutions.* New York: Oxford University Press, 1994

Calgary, City of. "Annexation Frequently Asked Questions." No. 3. www.calgary.ca/portal/server.pt/gateway/PTARGS_0_2_104_0 _0_35/http%3B/content.calgary.ca/CCA/City+Hall/Business+ Units/Development+and+Building+Approvals+and+Land+ Use+Planning+and+Policy/Land+Use+Planning/Current+ Studies+and+Ongoing+Activities/Annexation+Information/ Annexation+FAQ.htm#3/ (accessed 20 June 2007)

Canada. Statistics Canada. *2006 Census of Canada*

– Infrastructure Canada. *From Restless Communities to Resilient Places: Building a Stronger Future for All Canadians.* Final report of the External Advisory Committee on Cities and Communities. June 2006

Chapman, Tim. *The Congress of Vienna: Origins, Processes, and Results.* London: Routledge, 1998

Courchene, Thomas J. "Global Futures for Canada's Global Cities." *IRPP Policy Matters* 8, no. 2 (June 2007): 1–36

Dahl, Robert A. "The City in the Future of Democracy." *American Political Science Review* 41, no. 4 (1967): 953–70

Di Matteo, Livio, J.C. Herbert Emery, and Ryan English. "Is It Better to Live in a Basement or Get Your Own Place? Analysing the Costs and Benefits of Institutional Change for Northwestern Ontario." *Canadian Public Policy* 32, no. 2 (2006): 173–96

Dumont, Hugues, and Sébastien Van Drooghenbroeck. "The Status of Brussels in the Hypothesis of Confederalism." *Brussels Studies,* no. 10 (2007): 1–19. www.brusselsstudies.be/PDF/EN_46_BruS10 EN. pdf (accessed 8 February 2008)

Ebrahim-zadeh, Christine. "Back to Basics – Dutch Disease: Too Much Wealth Managed Unwisely." *Finance and Development: A Quarterly Magazine of the IMF* 40, no. 1 (2003). www.imf.org/external/pubs/ ft/fandd/2003/03/ebra.htm (accessed 5 December 2007)

Emery, J.C. Herbert, and Ronald D. Kneebone. *Should Alberta and Saskatchewan Unite?* Commentary no. 190. Toronto: C.D. Howe Institute, 2003

Faught, Jim. "Breaking Up Is Hard to Do: Explaining the 2002 San Fernando Valley Secession Vote." *Journal of Urban Affairs* 28, no. 4 (2006): 375–98

Fischel, William A. *The Homevoter Hypothesis: How Home Values Influence Local Government, School Finance, and Land-Use Policies.* Cambridge: Harvard University Press, 2001

Florida, Richard. "Wake up, Toronto – you're bigger than you think." *Globe and Mail* (Toronto), 27 October 2007, M1, M3

Frisken, Frances. *The Public Metropolis: The Political Dynamics of Urban Expansion in the Toronto Region, 1924–2003.* Toronto: Canadian Scholars' Press, 2007

Frug, Gerald E. *City Making: Building Communities without Building Walls.* Princeton: Princeton University Press, 1999

Gauvin, Monique, and Lizette Jalbert. "The Rise and Fall of the Parti Acadien." *Canadian Parliamentary Review* 10, no. 3 (1987). www.parl. gc.ca/Infoparl/english/index.htm?param=122/ (accessed 2 January 2008)

Gunlicks, Arthur B. *The Länder and German Federalism.* Manchester: Manchester University Press, 2003

Hall, Peter. *Theory and Practice of Regional Planning.* London: Pemberton Books, 1970

Harmack, David C. *Power and Society: Greater New York at the Turn of the Century.* New York: Russell Sage Foundation, 1982

Haussermann, Harmut. "Berlin." In *Metropolitan Governance and Spatial Planning: Comparative Case Studies of European City-Regions,* edited by William Salet, Andy Thornley, and Anton Kreukels, 113–24. London: Spon Press, 2003

Helleiner, Eric. *The Making of National Money: Territorial Currencies in Historical Perspective.* Ithaca, NY: Cornell University Press, 2003

Herbst, Jeffrey. *States and Power in Africa: Comparative Lessons in Authority and Control.* Princeton: Princeton University Press, 2000

Herrschel, Tassilo, and Peter Newman. *Governance of Europe's City Regions: Planning, Policy, and Politics.* London: Routledge, 2002

– "Global Competition and City Regional Governance in Europe." In *Regionalism Contested: Institution, Society and Governance,* edited by Iwona Sagan and Henrik Halkier, 203–22. Aldershot, England: Ashgate, 2005

Hill, Richard Child, and Kuniko Fujita. "The Nested City: Introduction." *Urban Studies* 40, no. 2 (2003): 207–17

Hooghe, Lisbet, and Gary Marks. "Unraveling the Central State, but How? Types of Multi-level Governance." *American Political Science Review* 97, no. 2 (2003): 233–43

Jackson, Robert. "Sovereignty and Its Presuppositions: 9/11 and After." *Political Studies* 55, no. 2 (2007): 297–317

Jacobs, Jane. *The Economy of Cities.* New York: Random House, 1969

– *Canadian Cities and Sovereignty Association.* Toronto: Canadian Broadcasting Corporation, 1980

– *Cities and the Wealth of Nations: Principles of Economic Life.* New York: Random House, 1984

Jonas, Andrew E.G., and Kevin Ward. "Introduction to a Debate on City-Regions: New Geographies of Governance, Democracy and Social Reproduction." *International Journal of Urban and Regional Research* 31, no. 1 (2007): 169–78

Judt, Tony. *Postwar: A History of Europe since 1945.* New York: Penguin, 2005

Keating, Michael. *Comparative Urban Politics: Power and the City in the United States, Canada, Britain and France.* Aldershot, Hants, UK: Edward Elgar, 1991

Keating, Michael, John Loughlin, and Kris Deschouwer. *Culture, Institutions, and Economic Development: A Study of Eight European Regions.* Cheltenham, UK: Edward Elgar, 2003

Keil, Roger, and Douglas Young. "A Charter for the People? A Research Note on the Debate about Municipal Autonomy in Toronto." *Urban Affairs Review* 39, no. 1 (2003): 87–102

Krasner, Stephen D. *Sovereignty: Organized Hypocrisy.* Princeton: Princeton University Press, 1999

Kresl, Peter Karl. *Planning Cities for the Future: The Successes and Failures of Urban Economic Strategies in Europe.* Cheltenham, UK: Edward Elgar, 2007

Kresl, Peter Karl, and Earl Fry. *The Urban Response to Internationalization.* Cheltenham, UK: Edward Elgar, 2005

Lagrou, Evert. "Brussels: A Superimposition of Social, Cultural, and Spatial Layers." In *Metropolitan Governance and Spatial Planning: Comparative Case Studies of European City-Regions,* edited by William Salet, Andy Thornley, and Anton Kreukels, 301–19. London: Spon Press, 2003

Leonardy, Uwe. "Territorial Reform of the Länder: A Demand of the Basic Law." In *German Public Policy and Federalism,* edited by Arthur B. Gunlicks, 65–90. New York: Berghahn Books, 2003

Locke, Wade, and Stephen G. Tomblin. *Good Governance, a Necessary but Not Sufficient Condition for Facilitating Economic Viability in a Peripheral Region: Cape Breton as a Case Study.* A discussion paper prepared for the Cape Breton Regional Municipality, October 2003. www.cbrm. ns.ca/portal/documents/GovernanceStudyReport. pdf (accessed 2 January 2008)

Loughlin, John. *Subnational Government: The French Experience.* Houndmills, Basingstoke, UK: Palgrave Macmillan, 2007

Macmillan, Margaret. *Paris 1919: Six Months That Changed the World.* New York: Random House, 2002

Magnusson, Warren. *The Search for Political Space: Globalization, Social Movements, and the Urban Political Experience.* Toronto: University of Toronto Press, 1996

Maldonado, Jesús Leal. "Metropolitan Government and Development Strategies in Madrid." In *Metropolitan Governance and Spatial*

Planning: Comparative Case Studies of European City-Regions, edited by William Salet, Andy Thornley, and Anton Kreukels, 359–74. London: Spon Press, 2003

Maritime Union Study. *The Report on Maritime Union Commissioned by the Governments of Nova Scotia, New Brunswick, and Prince Edward Island.* Fredericton: Queen's Printer, 1970

Masson, Jack, with Edward C. Lesage, Jr. *Alberta's Local Governments: Politics and Democracy.* Edmonton: University of Alberta Press, 1994

Murphy, Peter. *Preliminary 2006 Census Metropolitan Area and Census Agglomeration Delineation.* Research paper. Geography Working Paper Series. Ottawa: Statistics Canada, 2003

National Geographic Society. *The Historical Atlas of the United States.* Rev. ed. Washington, DC: National Geographic Society, 1993

Ohmae, Kenichi. *The End of the Nation State: The Rise of Regional Economies.* New York: Free Press, 1995

– *The Borderless World: Power and Strategy in the Interlinked Economy.* Rev. ed. New York: HarperBusiness, 1999

O'Leary, Brendan, Ian S. Lustick, and Thomas Callaghy, eds. *Rightsizing the State: The Politics of Moving Borders.* Oxford: Oxford University Press, 2007

Ontario. Task Force on the Future of Greater Toronto. *Greater Toronto: Report of the GTA Task Force.* Toronto: Queen's Printer, 1996

– Municipal Affairs and Housing. *Greenbelt Plan 2005*

– Public Infrastructure Renewal. *Growth Plan for the Greater Golden Horseshoe 2006*

Paal, Michaela. "Metropolitan Governance and Regional Planning in Vienna." In *Metropolitan Governance and Spatial Planning: Comparative Case Studies of European City-Regions,* edited by William Salet, Andy Thornley, and Anton Kreukels, 230–43. London: Spon Press, 2003

Parker, Geoffrey. *Sovereign City: The City-State through History.* London: Reaktion Books, 2004

Parker, Richard. "Calgary: A Uni-City at 50 Years." *Plan Canada* 45, no. 3 (2005): 29–31

Pavkovic, Aleksander, with Peter Radan. *Creating New States: Theory and Practice of Secession*. Aldershot, Hampshire, UK: Ashgate, 2007

Peirce, Neal R., with Curtis W. Johnson and John Stuart Hall. *Citistates: How America Can Prosper in a Competitive World*. Washington, DC: Seven Locks Press, 1993

Peters, Alfred H. "Manhattan: A Proposed New State." *American Journal of Politics* 2 (March 1893): 266–70

Peterson, Paul E. *City Limits*. Chicago: University of Chicago Press, 1981

Planhol, Xavier de, with Paul Claval. *An Historical Geography of France*. Translated by Janet Lloyd. Cambridge: Cambridge University Press, 1994

Public Policy Institute of New York State, Inc. *Could New York Let Upstate Be Upstate?* Albany, NY: Public Policy Institute of New York, 2004

Quebec. L'Assemblée nationale. *Débats*

– Task Force on Greater Montreal. *Montreal: A City-Region*. December 1993

– *Pacte 2000: Rapport de la Commission nationale sur les finances et la fiscalité locales*. 1999

Reniers, Matt. "Implementing the Draft Growth Plan in Brantford." Presentation to the third annual Insight Conference on Land Development and Planning in Ontario, 30 May 2006

Robson, Brian, et al. "Mapping City-Regions." A Framework for City-Regions. Working paper no. 1. London: Office of the Deputy Prime Minister, 2006

Rowe, Mary W. "Editor's Notes." *Ideas That Matter* 3, no. 1 (2003): 2

Sancton, Andrew. "Jane Jacobs on the Organization of Municipal Government." *Journal of Urban Affairs* 22, no. 4 (2000): 463–71

– *Merger Mania: The Assault on Local Government*. Montreal and Kingston: McGill-Queen's University Press, 2000

– "Fusions et défusions municipales au Québec et en Ontario." In *Le parti Libéral: Enquête sur les réalisations du gouvernement Charest*, edited by François Pétry, Éric Bélanger, and Louis M. Imbeau, 321–38. Quebec: Les Presses de l'Université Laval, 2006

Sassen, Saskia. *The Global City: New York, London, Tokyo*. 2nd ed. Princeton: Princeton University Press, 2001

– *Territory · Authority · Rights: From Medieval to Global Assemblages*. Princeton: Princeton University Press, 2006

Savitch, H.V., and Ronald K. Vogel. "Suburbs without a City: Power and City-County Consolidation." *Urban Affairs Review* 39, no. 6 (2004): 758–90

Schwab, Brigitte, and Daniel Kubler. "Metropolitan Governance and the 'Democratic Deficit': Theoretical Issues and Empirical Findings." Paper presented at the "Area-Based Initiatives in Contemporary Urban Policy" conference, Danish Building and Urban Research and European Urban Research Association, Copenhagen, 17–19 May 2001

Sellers, Jeffery M. *Governing from Below: Urban Regions and the Global Economy*. New York: Cambridge University Press, 2002

Sharpe, L.J. "The Failure of Local Government Modernization in Britain: A Critique of Functionalism." *Canadian Public Administration* 24, no. 1 (1981): 92–115

– ed. *The Government of World Cities: The Future of the Metro Model*. Chichester, UK: John Wiley, 1995

Sonenshein, Raphael D. *The City at Stake: Secession, Reform, and the Battle for Los Angeles*. Princeton: Princeton University Press, 2004

Spruyt, Hendrik. *The Sovereign State and Its Competitors: An Analysis of Systems Change*. Princeton: Princeton University Press, 1994

Stevenson, Don. "Possible Regional Implications of a New City of Toronto Act." In Broadbent et al., *Towards a New City of Toronto Act*, 27–9

Taylor, Peter J. "World Cities and Territorial States: The Rise and Fall of Their Mutuality." In *World Cities in a World-System*, edited by

Paul L. Knox and Peter J. Taylor, 48–62. Cambridge: Cambridge University Press, 1995.

Ternhorst, Peter, and Jacques van de Ven. "Territorialisation of the State and Urban Trajectories: Amsterdam and Brussels Compared." In *The Territorial Factor: Political Geography in a Changing World*, edited by Gertjan Dijkink and Hans Knippenberg, 399–428. Amsterdam: Vossius Press, 2001

Toronto, City of. Office of the Chief Administrative Officer, Strategic and Corporate Policy Division. "Powers of Canadian Cities: The Legal Framework." Internal report. June 2000

Travers, Tony. *The Politics of London: Governing an Ungovernable City.* Houndmills, Basingstoke, UK: Palgrave Macmillan, 2004

United States. Office of Management and Budget. "Standards for Defining Metropolitan and Micropolitan Statistical Areas." *Federal Register*, part 9, 27 December 2000, 82228–38

– *OMB Bulletin*, 22 February 2005

Ward, Peter M. "The Successful Management and Administration of World Cities: Mission Impossible?" In *World Cities in a World-System*, edited by Paul L. Knox and Peter J. Taylor, 298–314. Cambridge: Cambridge University Press, 1995

Wellman, Christopher Heath. *A Theory of Secession: The Case for Political Self-Determination.* Cambridge: Cambridge University Press, 2005

White, Richard. *The Growth Plan for the Greater Golden Horseshoe in Historical Perspective.* Paper 4. Neptis Papers on Growth in the Toronto Metropolitan Region. Toronto, December 2007

Young, Robert A. *The Secession of Quebec and the Future of Canada.* Montreal and Kingston: McGill-Queen's University Press, 1995

– "Secession as Revolution." *Homo Oeconomicus* 21, no. 2 (2004): 373–95

Map References

Note: Maps not listed below were derived from material in the public domain.

Map 2: Copenhagen and its links with Malmo, Sweden (large-scale map)

– ESRI Data and Maps Media Kit, Europe Directory. Redlands, California. Environmental Systems Research Institute Inc., 2006.

Map 3: The province of Ontario showing the Greater Golden Horseshoe

– Statistics Canada. *Census of Canada 2006. Census Division Census Metropolitan Area: Maps* [machine readable datafile]. Ottawa: Statistics Canada, 2006.

– DMTI Spatial Inc. DMTI Canadian Atlas Map Bundle Vers. 1. Markham, ON, 2005.

– ESRI Data & Maps and StreetMap USA. Redlands California. Environmental Systems Research Institute Inc., 2006.

Map 4: The Greater Golden Horseshoe and other Toronto-related boundaries

– Ontario Ministry of Public Infrastructure Renewal. *Places to Grow: Better Choices. Brighter Future* – Growth Plan for the Greater

Golden Horseshoe. Schedule 1: Greater Golden Horseshoe Growth Plan Area, 2006.

Map 5: The Montreal CMA and the territory of the Montreal Metropolitan Community (MMC)

– Statistics Canada. 2008. "Montreal CMA – Percentage of Population Aged 14 Years and under by 2006 Census Subdivision" (map). *2006 Census: Analysis Series. Maps.*

http://www12.statcan.ca/english/census06/analysis/agesex/maps/Montreal_Age14%20CSD_Ec_v01.pdf (accessed February 5, 2008).

– Communauté métropolitaine de Montréal, Territoire de la Communauté métropolitaine de Montréal, July 2002.

Index